DL 138

Marine
Science 2

Written by **Lisa Wood**
Illustrated by **Stephanie O'Shaughnessy**

Edited by **Dianne Draze** and **Sonsie Conroy**

ISBN 1-883055-46-6
© Copyright 2001 **Dandy Lion Publications**
All rights reserved.

For more information about Dandy Lion Publications, visit our website
www.dandylionbooks.com

Table of Contents

Scientific Resources and Books for Students 4
Introduction for Teachers 5

1. Bringing the Sea Inside . . . .
   Setting Up an Aquarium 6

2. Ecosystems – The Kelp Forest
   Background Information 9
   Activities 11
   Worksheets 15

3. What is Sea Water?
   Background Information 17
   Activities 18
   Worksheets 22

4. Fish and Sharks
   Background Information 24
   Activities 27
   Worksheets 31

5. Marine Mammals
   Background Information 34
   Activities 35
   Worksheets 39
   Picture Cards 44

6. Invertebrates
   Background Information 54
   Activities 56
   Worksheets 60
   Picture Cards 64

7. Marine Plants and Algae
   Background Information 75
   Activities 76
   Worksheets 78

8. Food Chains and Webs
   Background Information 80
   Activities 81
   Worksheets 83

Glossary 86
Answers 88

Scientific Resources

Carolina Biological Supply
2700 York Street
Burlington, NC 27215
800-334-5551

Ward's Natural Science
P.O. Box 92913
Rochester, NY 14692
716-359-2502

Frey Scientific
905 Hickory Lane
Mansfield, OH 44905
419-589-9905

Marine reference
The Marine Aquarium Reference
written by Martin A Moe, Jr.
published by Green Turtle Publications

Suggested Books for Students

A Swim Through the Sea - Joy Pratt
A Symphony of Whales - Steve Schuch
Big Blue Whale - Nicola Davies
Davy's Dream - Paul Owen Lewis
Dolphins at Daybreak - Mary Pope Osborne
Dory Story - Jerry Pallotta
Follow the Moon - Sarah Weeks
Hungry, Hungry Sharks - Joanna Cole
In the Swim: Poems and Paintings - Douglas Florian
Into the Sea - Alix Berenzy
The Iceberg - Takamado No Miya Hisako
Song - Sheryl McFarlane
My Life With the Wave - Catherine Cowan
Sharks! (All Aboard Book) - Lynn Wilsons
Swimmy - Leo Lionni
The Magic School Bus on the Ocean Floor - Joanna Cole
The Sea-Thing Child - Russell Hoban
The Wild Whale Watch - Eva Moore

Books for older students/advanced readers

20,000 Leagues Under the Sea - Jules Verne
A Dolphin Named Bob - Twig C. George
Buoy: Home at Sea - Bruce Balan
Captain Jim and the Killer Whales - Carol A. Amato
How to Speak Dolphin in Three Easy Lessons - Dan Greenburg
Hurricane: Open Seas, 1844 (Survival, No 9) - Kathleen Duey
Island of the Blue Dolphins - Scott O'Dell
Mystery of the Dolphin Detective - Elspeth Campbell Murphy
Sea Otter Inlet - Celia Godkin
Seabird - Clancy Holling
The Adventures of Phokey the Sea Otter: Based on a True Story - Marianne Riedman
The Music of Dolphins - Karen Hesse
The Sunbeam and the Wave - Harriet Elizabeth Hamilton
The Wanderer - Sharon Creech

Introduction for Teachers

 The Ocean

The ocean and its inhabitants have been a favorite course of study for students of all ages. Marine science, the study of the ocean, the creatures that live within, and the processes that shape it, holds a special wonder that sparks the imagination and stirs a sense of adventure. Since the ocean is not our natural home, it is not as familiar to us as many other topics of study – therein lies the wonder. Scientists have been studying the ocean and the animals that live in it for centuries, yet even today, in the age of technology, there are still regions of the ocean that we know little about and strange new species of animals that are yet to be discovered.

 About This Book

This book will allow teachers to guide intermediate grade students through a series of scientific experiments and cross-curricular activities in marine science. A scientific background is not necessary. Information on all the topics is included so that teachers can introduce their classes to the activities without having to perform their own detailed research.

There are three books in this series, each designed for different grade levels. In addition, each book focuses on a different marine ecosystem:

- **Book 1** (grades K-2) - the tide pool
- **Book 2** (grades 3-5) - the kelp forest
- **Book 3** (grades 6-8) - the coral reef

While each book focuses on one particular ecosystem, the information and activities presented in each book encompass other areas of the ocean as well.

Each topic contains background information for teachers, experiments or activities and follow-up questions aimed at leading students into thinking critically about the activities.

Each activity or experiment is designed to stand alone or to be used in connection with others in a marine science unit. It may also be helpful to supplement these lessons with books or videos about the ocean from your school or public library. At the end of the book is a glossary, defining many of the scientific words used in the book. You may want to use these words as spelling or vocabulary words during the unit.

 Equipment

The equipment needed for each activity has been kept simple. Most items can be found in your classroom or at a local store. A list of scientific suppliers has also been included on page 4 in case you need to order any additional supplies. For some of the supplies, such as shoe boxes, it is often possible to have the students supply their own.

 If You Can Visit the Ocean

If you live by the ocean, a field trip to a local tide pool or beach at the end of the marine science unit will give students a hands-on experience with the topics that they have been studying. At the end of each section you will find field study activities that can be done at the beach, or in the classroom after a visit to the beach. Since student transportation is often difficult to arrange, check to see if you can legally collect items from the beach and bring them into the classroom. Some specimens can be collected without a permit in most states. It may also be possible, after obtaining a permit, to collect live specimens at the ocean and keep them in the classroom for the students to observe. Please check your local laws concerning collection of marine organisms before you take anything from the beach.

Chapter 1

Bringing the Sea Inside

Setting Up an Aquarium

Having a classroom fish tank is an excellent way to add to your study of marine science. It gives students the ability to observe marine (or fresh water) fish up close. Once set up, an aquarium can be easily maintained for many years. The students can continue their observations and care of the aquarium long after the ocean unit is completed.

Salt Water or Fresh Water

The first decision to make before setting up an aquarium is whether to use fresh water or salt water. Both fresh water aquariums and salt water aquariums have their benefits. In general, fresh water aquariums are easier and cheaper to set up and maintain, while salt water aquariums allow for more exotic, colorful fish. For a classroom aquarium that will not take much time to maintain and that will allow for student participation, a fresh water aquarium is recommended. The following are instructions for setting up a fresh water aquarium. If you wish to set up a salt water aquarium consider investing in a book (like *The Marine Aquarium Reference*, see page 4) that will take you through the set-up step by step.

How To Set Up an Aquarium

What Kind of Tank?

The first part of an aquarium system is the tank. When looking for a tank the two things to keep in mind are size and material. You can purchase tanks ranging in size from half-gallon to over 100 gallons, though a rectangular tank between 5 and 20 gallons works best for classroom use. Tanks are made either out of glass or Plexiglas. A glass tank is often less expensive and easier to maintain, while a Plexiglas tank allows for better initial viewing

(Plexiglas is easily scratched, and the clarity of the tank may diminish over time). Whichever tank you purchase, make sure it has a well-fitting lid in order to slow the process of evaporation.

Filter system and other materials

The next piece of equipment you need is a filter system. For short term use an under-gravel filter with an external air-pump works well. For any long term use or for a salt water aquarium, an external filter-pump system such as an *Aquaclear* or *Magnum* system is recommended. With an under-gravel filter system you will need filter plates, risers, replaceable charcoal filter media cartridges, air tubing, air stones and an air pump. These materials are often sold as a set. External filter-pump systems are self-contained and often come with filter media that can be replaced periodically.

Other materials that you will need are a lid for the tank, lights, gravel, a thermometer and a heater.* It is also a good idea to purchase a fish net, plants and a scrubbing pad for algae (pads for glass tanks are typically dark blue and pads for Plexiglas tanks are usually white.)

* This might not be necessary if you are in a warm climate or plan to have fish that can tolerate cold water.

Setting up the aquarium

Once you have all the materials, it is time to set up the aquarium.

- Place the aquarium near an electrical outlet so that you can plug in the pump and light.
- Before you add water, set up the tank, filter and gravel. If you are using an external filter-pump system, all you have to do is mount it on the side of your tank and plug it in to begin use (never plug in a filter-pump system before adding water to the pump).
- The gravel can then be added to the bottom of the tank. It is always good to wash the gravel before adding water to eliminate any dirt or dust from your tank.
- If you are using an under-gravel filter system, lay the filter plates on the bottom of the tank and then add the risers (plastic cylinders) into each corner. Add the gravel on top of the filter plates once the risers are in place.
- Attach an air stone to the end of a piece of air tubing and insert it into the riser, placing the top containing the filter cartridge on top. If you wish to use two air stones, one in each corner, you will need to connect the two pieces of tubing with a T-shaped connector. From this connector you can run another length of tubing to your external air pump.

Adding water

Now you are ready to add water to your tank. For a fresh water tank, it is best to use filtered water since regular tap water will cause mineral deposits and algae growth. With any type of water you need to use a water conditioner to eliminate chlorine. Water conditioners can be purchased at any pet store that carries fish.

Salt water can be made by adding sea salt to filtered water. Sea salt is different from the salt used for cooking and can also be purchased from a pet store. One brand is *Instant Ocean*. If you live near the ocean, you can also simply collect water from the ocean, but make sure you are collecting from a non-contaminated area. Normal sea water has 34 parts per thousand salt, or 4 tablespoons per gallon.

The best way to get your aquarium ready for fish is to add a cup of water from an existing aquarium and allow it to run through the filters for a few days in order to establish a healthy bacteria level. If you do not have access to any other aquariums from which you can borrow water, you will want to make sure that the first fish you add to the aquarium are very hearty. You can also increase the fishes' survival by adding the water your fish came in from the fish store to your tank.

Selecting Fish

Now you are ready to add fish to your aquarium. When choosing fish, make sure that they are compatible. If you get an aggressive chiclid and a peaceful platy, you will be observing predation firsthand in  the classroom. Most good pet stores will be able to tell you which fish are compatible. Often it is good to get several of the same small fish so that they can form schools. The general rule for the number of fish in a tank is one fish per gallon for small fish and one fish per two gallons if they are medium to large fish. It is always best to have too few fish and allow them to have lots of room to swim than to have too many fish that are crowded.

Many people have bought fish and brought them home only to have them die in their tank within a few days. If this happens, take the fish and a sample of water back to the store. Most pet stores will refund your money or give you a new fish. They will also check your water to make sure nothing is wrong in your tank.

Caring for the Aquarium

You will need to feed your fish 2 to 3 times a week. When you select the fish at the pet store, also select a fish food. Most fish will eat flake food, though more exotic fish need special diets. You should only feed the fish as much as they will consume in a few minutes. Extra food will fall to the bottom and cause excess algae growth. You can also purchase feeder tablets that will allow a small amount of food to be released over time. These are good for short vacations when you will not be in the classroom.

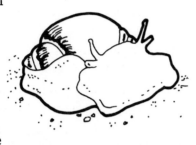

One problem that occurs in many tanks is algae growth. The best way to take care of algae growth is to get aquatic snails from the pet store to live in your tank. Not only do they keep the tank clean, but they often reproduce by laying small egg packets on the side of the tank. Students can watch the snails eggs grow and hatch if they are removed from the tank (inside the tank the fish often eat them). If you do not want to use snails, the tank will need to be cleaned with an algae pad every week or two.

You will also need to change the filter medium every three to six months. Partial water changes (taking out a few gallons and replacing them with clean water) are also needed every month. Make sure that every time you add new water, you also add water conditioner. If you want to keep extra care of your tank, you can also check the pH level of the water. Kits containing pH strips are available at pet stores. These can be used simply by putting a drop of water on the strip. The pH of your fish tank should be between 6.8 and 7.2.

How Students Can Participate

Students can participate in setting up the aquarium and caring for the fish. Groups of students can share the responsibility of feeding the fish, cleaning the tank, checking the pH, and changing the water.

Ecosystems

The Kelp Forest

Background Information

Ecology is the scientific study of the relationships among organisms in the same environment. It involves all aspects of the organisms' environment, both living and non-living. An **environment** is the external surroundings of an organism, while an **ecosystem** is a term used to describe an environmental unit that consists of living and nonliving parts, interacting to form a stable system. While an ecosystem consists of many animals and plants living together in the same environment, a **habitat** is the living place (home) of one specific organism, characterized by its physical and biological properties.

So if we were to say that an owl lives in a tree, that is its habitat. If we were to describe the tree in terms of its physical properties, the temperature, height of tree, type of tree, soil type, etc., we would be describing the owl's environment. And if we were to describe all the other creatures that live in and around that tree as well as the physical environment such as temperature, wind, light, soil, and how these interact, we would be describing an ecosystem.

It is important that no animal or plant lives alone. They are all part of an ecosystem that includes air, water, soil, light, temperature, and all the other organisms that live in the ecosystem. All put together, the ecosystem works like a finely tuned machine that keeps all its components in balance. If one piece of the ecosystem is disturbed or damaged, the entire ecosystem could be put in jeopardy.

The Kelp Forest

The ecosystem that this book will focus on is the kelp forest. While you will find that not all activities are focused on the kelp forest, it is a theme that runs throughout the book. You can use this as the focus of your unit on the ocean or as just one part of a unit on the entire ocean.

Kelp is a term used to describe several species of large brown seaweed. Kelp is a type of algae, a plant-like organism that is found in the ocean. Kelp grows in dense patches in the rocky near-shore environment. Because kelp grows upward from the ocean floor to the ocean's surface, its long, swaying fronds resemble a forest of trees. Kelp grows at depths from two meters to thirty meters. Kelp is fast growing and in southern California can grow thirty centimeters per day. Although individual kelp plants can live up to seven years, their life span may be reduced due to storms when entire plants or parts of the plants are ripped apart and washed ashore by strong water motion.

Kelp forests are found in cold, nutrient-rich water. While the kelp forest is one of the most biologically productive habitats in the ocean, the larger forests are restricted to areas where the sea water temperature never rises above 20 degrees Celsius. Kelp forests are found in the Arctic and Antarctic as well as in Britain, the north Pacific from Japan east to California, in the western Atlantic southward to Cape Cod, and in Australia.

Features of Kelp

Kelp has four basic features: the stipe, blade, holdfast and air bladder.

The **stipe** is a flexible tube that has a similar function as a stem or trunk on a plant or tree. The stipe is strong and connects the other parts of the kelp together.

The **blade** is like a leaf, but it is leathery and often has ridges that run its length. The blade is the primary piece of the kelp to carry out photosynthesis. The blade can carry out photosynthesis on both of its surfaces, unlike a land plant that only uses the top surface for photosynthesis.

The **holdfast** looks similar to the roots of a land plant, but it acts in a different manner. While roots are used for stabilizing a plant and collecting nutrients from the soil, the holdfast is used only to anchor the kelp onto the rocky sea floor. The kelp is able to absorb all its nutrients directly from the surrounding water.

At the base of every blade is a round ball filled with gas, this is the **air bladder**. The air bladders help the kelp float. The air bladders on bull kelp can be as large as soccer balls. With thousands of air bladders, the kelp reaches towards the top of the ocean as it grows. Once it reaches the surface, the kelp grows along the surface, forming a canopy that shades the waters below.

This top layer of the kelp forest is called the **canopy layer**. The area around the rocky floor is called the **floor layer**, and the area in between is the **middle layer**. Different animals live in each of these layers. By far, the

floor layer of the kelp forest is home to the widest variety of creatures. A single holdfast can house thousands of animals from a wide variety of phyla. In and around the holdfast you can find sponges, worms, shrimp, crabs, snails, brittle stars, sea squirts, anemones, cup coral, bryozoans and sea urchins, as well as a variety of bottom-dwelling fish such as swell sharks, halibut and rock fish. In the middle layer you can find a large number of invertebrates living on the stipes and blades of the kelp such as bryozoans, crabs, snails and slugs. In the middle layer you can also find jellyfish, señorita fish, surfperch, blacksmith, seals and sea lions. The canopy layer also holds many of these same animals as well as sea otters in the Pacific Ocean.

For more information about algae, see Chapter 7.

Chapter Concepts

The main focus of this chapter is the kelp forest as an ecosystem that supports many forms of sea life. The specific concepts presented in each lesson are:

2.1 - Relating an organism to an environment

2.2 - A graphic representation of organisms in an ecosystem

2.3 - Introduction to animals that live in the kelp forest

2.4 - A review of different ecosystems, comparing similarities and differences

2.5 - Animal-plant dependency demonstration

2.6 - Comparison of the animals that live in a kelp forest and in a tide pool

Ecosystems

Activities

Some students will be able to complete the following activities best when thinking of environments and ecosystems that are familiar to them, that they have seen in their own experiences. Other students will be able to build the concepts of ecosystems around environments that may not be as familiar to them, such as the kelp forest. These activities can be performed at either of these conceptual levels, or moving from familiar to foreign. Some of the activities in this chapter are similar to ones offered in the first book, but it is expected that students at this grade level will give more detailed, sophisticated responses.

2.1 From Organism to Ecosystem

Overview
In this activity, students will differentiate between organisms, environments and ecosystem.

Materials
- ✓ "From Organism to Ecosystem" worksheet
- ✓ pencils or pens
- ✓ paper

Procedure
1. Using information from the Background Information discuss the differences between organisms, environments, and ecosystems.

2. Hand out the "From Organism to Ecosystem" worksheet and have students choose an organism and write the name of the organism in the box at the top of the page.

3. Next have the students describe where the animal lives. Have them concentrate on the physical properties of the environment (air, temperature, light, water, etc.).

4. Next have them list other plants and animals that live in this same environment. Also have them think about what their organism might eat and what its predators are. Fill these elements in on the worksheets.

5. Once they have finished describing all the components of their animal's ecosystem, give them an opportunity to illustrate the ecosystem.

2.2 Environment Mind Map

Overview
In this activity, students will create a mind map on an environment by brainstorming what they know about an environment. The students will do this activity in cooperative groups.

Materials
- ✓ large paper
- ✓ pencils or markers

Procedure
1. Review how to do a mind map by writing the main topic in the center of the paper and attaching related ideas with lines.

2. Divide students into small groups. Assign or have each group choose one of the following environments:

lake	meadow
forest	mountains
river	tide pool
kelp forest	desert
open ocean	pond

3. Give each group a large piece of paper and have them write the ecosystem in a circle in the center of the paper. Then they should write as many animals and plants as they can think of that live in that environment and connect each organism to the environment with a line. They may first list general categories (like mammals) and then connect specific examples (like whales and seals) to the general categories.

4. Have each group display and explain their ecosystem.

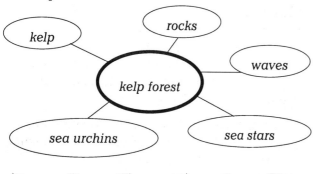

2.3 Who Lives in the Kelp Forest?

Overview
In this cross-curricular activity students will explore how different animals are adapted to live in kelp.

Materials
✓ color pictures of kelp forest animals

Procedure
1. Collect color pictures of animals that live in the kelp forest, either from books in your library or from the Internet. Use animals such as kelp fish, kelp crabs, sting rays, leopard sharks and turban snails.

2. Show students the pictures and discuss how each animal is adapted to its environment.

3. Then have each student choose an animal and, if necessary, do more research on the animal. Then they should write a haiku or free form poem about the animal.

4. To add complexity to this assignment, you can have the poems be in the shape of the animal that they describe.

2.4 Group Project: Ecosystems

Overview
In this activity groups of students will research different ecosystems and make a presentation to the class. This lesson could be used in place of Lesson 2.2, or you can use both lessons as a way to reinforce the concept of ecosystems.

Materials
✓ paper
✓ pencils and pens
✓ reference materials
✓ poster board
✓ glue

Procedure
1. Break the class into groups of 3 to 4 students. Assign each group an ecosystem or let them choose their own. Some suggestions are a pond, forest, meadow, river, or tide pool.

2. Give the students ample time to research their ecosystem. They may need several days to complete this task. Have them use resources such as the school library or the Internet to find information on their ecosystems.

3. Have each group prepare a poster, chart, mural, or booklet that illustrates all the information that they have gathered. Encourage them to use illustrations as well as text.

4. Once all the groups are finished putting together their posters, have each group teach the class about their ecosystem.

5. You can have each group suggest a question about their presentation that could be used on a quiz at the end of the project.

2.5 Plant-Animal Dependence

Overview
This demonstration will show how plants and animals in an ecosystem are dependent on one another. This should be done as a class demonstration and discussion.

Materials
- ✓ three test tubes
- ✓ aquatic plants
- ✓ snails
- ✓ water

Procedure
1. Prepare three test tubes by putting water in all three. In one put an aquatic plant. In the second put a water snail. In the third put an aquatic plant and a snail. Seal the top of all three tubes.

2. Show the tubes to students and ask them which ecosystem will sustain life longest? Since there is no new oxygen or carbon dioxide entering the closed system, how long will it be before the plant dies without carbon dioxide or the snail dies from lack of oxygen?

3. Discuss the fact that plants need carbon dioxide (which is produced by animals like fish and invertebrates like the snail) and animals need oxygen (which is produced by plants). In an ecosystem that includes both plants and animals, there is an exchange of oxygen and carbon dioxide so that all organisms get what they need.

4. After the discussion, take the plants and the snails out of the test tubes so that they do not die.

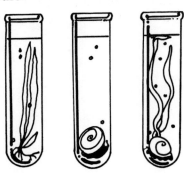

2.6 Ecosystem Comparison

Overview
This lesson uses a Venn diagram to compare animals that live in two different marine environments.

Materials
- ✓ "Ecosystem Comparison" worksheet

Procedure
1. Discuss the fact that tide pools and kelp forests are two important marine environments that have an abundance of organisms. Many of these organisms can be found in both places.

2. List or have students research some animals that live in kelp forests and also some that live in tide pools.

3. Give students the worksheet on page 16 and have them complete it by listing animals that reside in the kelp forest, those that are found in tide pools, and the animals that can be found in both places.

4. Discuss what about the two ecosystems make them ideal environments for the animals that live in both places. What are the animals' needs? How are these needs met in these environments?

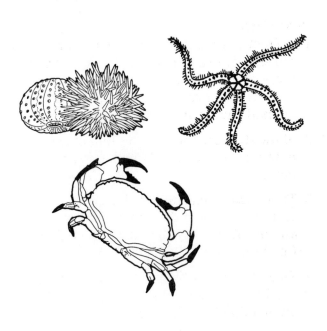

If You Live by the Ocean

If you live by the ocean you may have the opportunity to visit a kelp forest first hand. In areas where kelp forests occur, kelp can often be found washed up on the beach. Make sure to check your local tide charts to pick a time when the tide is low. If you go at high tide, the students may not be able to approach the beach and find kelp. If you find clumps of fresh kelp washed up on the beach you can inspect it to find animals still attached. Inspect the blades and stipes carefully, as well as the holdfast. With a little effort you can break apart the holdfast and hopefully discover many animals. After you have taken a good look at any animals you find on the kelp, have the students return the animals to the ocean. Make sure to tell students that all the creatures are alive and that they must be very careful about handling these fragile creatures. Also be aware that in most states it is illegal to take any animals from the beach without the proper permits (these are different from fishing permits).

Follow-Up Questions/Activities

- What physical stresses might an animal that lives in a kelp forest have to deal with that another ocean or land animal might not?

- What are some adaptations kelp forest animals might have for living in such a dynamic environment?

- Create a kelp forest as an art project using a bulletin board or wall of the classroom. You can add kelp using string for stipes and holdfasts and paper for the blades. As your studies progress through the ocean unit, create and add organisms such as sea stars, octopuses, sea otters and urchins to your kelp forest.

- Why would the kelp forest be a good place to live? For what kinds of animals would it be a bad place to live?

- How does the kelp forest compare to ___ (some other ecosystem)?

- Make a vertical drawing that shows three layers of the kelp forest. Label the levels and add the animals that live in each level.

- Choose music and write an introduction to a documentary film on the kelp forest.

From Organism to Ecosystem

Name _____

My Organism

The Environment

This is what it is like in the environment where my organism lives _____

_____

_____

Other Organisms

These are some of the plants and animals that also live in that environment.

_____   _____

_____   _____

_____   _____

_____   _____

Prey and Predators

This is what my organism eats_____

_____

These are its predators_____

_____

The Ecosystem

All together these components
make up the ecosystem called

Ecosystem Comparison

Name _____

Write the names of the animals that live in the kelp forest or in the tide pool in the correct circle. In the center write the names of the animals that live in both places.

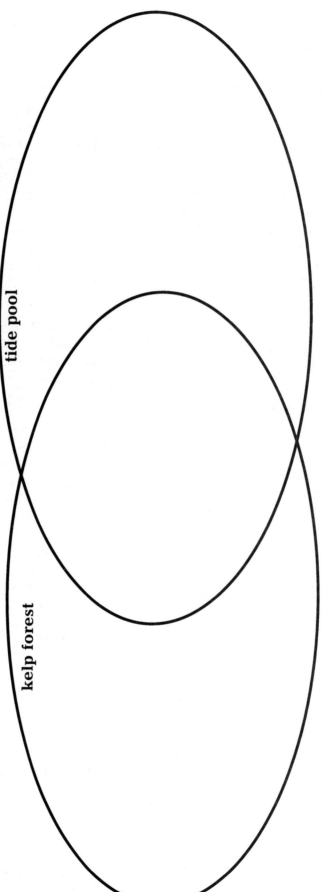

tide pool

kelp forest

What conclusions can you draw about the animals that live in both environments? _____

_____

_____

16

Chapter 3

What is Sea Water?

Understanding Density

Background Information

The earth is virtually covered in water. Nearly ¾ of the earth's surface is covered in water, 97% of this water lying in the oceans. Without this much water, earth would most likely resemble our nearest neighbor, Mars, a dry, lifeless planet. The concept of sea water and how it differs from fresh water can be hard to grasp if you have never been to the ocean, as many people have not. Through these activities students will learn about sea water and some of its properties.

Sea Water

How salty is sea water? Sea water is approximately 3.4 % or 34 parts per thousand (ppt) salt. This means that for every thousand molecules of water, there are 34 molecules of salt. The **salinity** (how much salt is in the water) of sea water is very consistent throughout the world's oceans. The highest ocean salinity is found in the Red Sea where it reaches 39 ppt, and the lowest is near the North Pole where it is only 32 ppt during the summer when the icebergs melt. This range is quite small in comparison to many lakes and rivers, which can vary from near 0 ppt to over 40 ppt in some isolated lakes. The reason that the salinity of the world's oceans is nearly the same is because of the constant moving of water between oceans through global ocean currents.

Density

One property of sea water that you will study is density. **Density** is an object's mass per unit area, while weight is simply an object's mass. And since sea water has more dissolved solids in its liquid matrix than fresh water does, it has a higher density.

What this means is that a liter of salt water is heavier than a liter of fresh water. A bottle of salt water will sink in fresh water, while a bottle of fresh water will float in salt water (as long as the bottle itself is not to heavy).

Temperature also affects water density. Cold water is denser than warm water. This means that cold water will sink beneath warm water.

Common Questions

This always brings up the question, "If you have warm salty water and cold fresh water, which one will be denser?" The answer is; it depends on how salty and how warm or cold the water is. In this unit students will have the opportunity to test this out for themselves.

Another question that arises when learning about density is; "Why do icebergs float?" Icebergs form at the polar regions of the earth's oceans where the air temperature can drop well below freezing. While fresh water freezes at 0° C, salt water freezes at -1.9° C. Icebergs are actually fresh water even though they exist in the ocean. As sea water freezes, the salt falls out of the water-salt matrix and sinks. So while icebergs are fresh water, the salt water below them can be very salty and very dense. In fact, over 75% over the earth's fresh water is trapped in glaciers and icebergs. Ice is less dense than water, as we see with a glass of ice water; the ice floats near the surface of the fresh water because it is less dense than the water.

Chapter Contents

The main concept presented in this chapter is that sea water has properties that are different than fresh water; therefore, it behaves differently than fresh water. The concepts presented in the lessons are:

3.1 - Density of salt water

3.2 - Density of hot and cold water

3.3 - Developing a hypothesis about water density and testing it

3.4 - Differences in freezing rates between fresh and salt water

3.5 - Why icebergs float

17

What is Sea Water?

Many of these activities will use both fresh water and water with salt added to it. The salt water does not have to be the same salinity as the ocean. For some of these activities you may want to add food coloring to one of the two types of water. This will make it easier for you and the students to tell the difference between the two types of water.

3.1 Using Weight to Compare Density

Overview
In this experiment students will perform experiments that demonstrate water density and how the salinity of water changes water density. This can be done as a demonstration or in small groups.

Materials
- ✓ balance
- ✓ water
- ✓ salt
- ✓ several containers (large light ones work best)
- ✓ measuring cup
- ✓ paper
- ✓ pencils

Procedure
1. Divide students into small groups.

2. Prepare several different concentrations of salt water and one with fresh water. You will want to make at least one of the salt waters samples very salty.

3. Have the students take their empty containers and weigh them and record the weights. You will need to have some way to identify each container if they look the same, such as a label on a piece of tape.

4. Next have students put an equal volume of the different concentrations of water into the different containers. They must be exact in measuring the equal volumes. Using a larger volume of water will make it easier to measure the differences in weights.

5. Weigh the filled containers and record the new weights. Once the students have done this they need to subtract the weight of the empty container from the weight of the filled container to get the weight of the water. They can also calculate density by using the formula:
density = weight/volume.

6. Now that the students know the weights of the water, they can tell which one has the most salt. The more salt, the more dense the water. Since the containers hold the same volume, any difference in weight will be a result of the difference in their densities.

3.2 Warm Water vs. Cold Water

Overview
In this lesson students will experiment with the difference in density between cold and warm water.

Materials
- ✓ two small beakers (or jars)
- ✓ two large beakers (or jars)
- ✓ string
- ✓ water
- ✓ ice cubes
- ✓ hot water
- ✓ food coloring

Procedure

1. Begin by preparing a batch of very warm water along with very cold water. You can use ice cubes to cool the water. Ask students to develop a hypothesis about what will happen when hot and cold water are combined.

2. Tie a string around the top of each small beaker so that you have a length on either side to hold on to (see illustration). Fill each of the small beakers to the top with water, one cold and one warm. Add a different color of food coloring to each of the small beakers.

3. Fill each of the large beakers ¾ full with water, one with warm and one with cold. Make sure to leave enough room for the volume of the small beaker to be contained without over-flowing.

4. Carefully lower the small beaker of cold water into the large container of warm water and observe what happens.

5. Then carefully lower the small beaker of warm water into the large container of cold water and watch what happens.

6. Discuss what happened and why — cold water is denser than hot water.

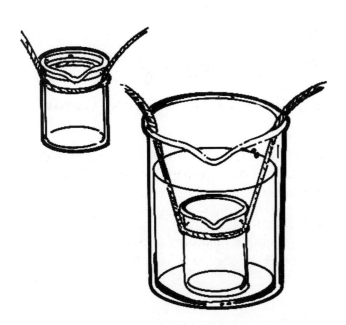

3.3 Experiments with Density

Overview

In this activity groups of students will be able to design and perform their own set of experiments using the setup of the previous experiment. They will be testing the differences in density between hot and cold and between fresh and salty water.

Materials

✓ "Water Density" worksheet
✓ large and small beakers
✓ string
✓ measuring spoons
✓ thermometers
✓ water
✓ salt
✓ food coloring
✓ ice

Procedure

1. Tell students that they will be designing experiments to test their theories about water density. Review the first two experiments. Have students pose questions about hot and cold and fresh and salty water that they could answer with a new experiment. Sample questions might be:
   • Is cold salty water denser that hot salty water?
   • What happens when hot salty water interacts with cold fresh water?
   • Is the density of salt water in direct proportion to the amount of salt in it?
   • Is very cold water denser than moderately cold water?

2. Give each team of students a copy of the worksheet. Have them fill out their hypothesis before you give them the equipment. Once they have decided on the experiment they are going to perform, have them write out their procedure, being as precise as they can be and being sure to indicate how much salt they will use and/or how hot their water will be.

3. Once they have performed the experiments have them fill out the results and conclusions sections of the worksheet.

4. If there is time, you can have the groups do another experiment and record it on another copy of the worksheet.

3.4 Making Icebergs

Overview
In this experiment the students will observe the different freezing temperatures of fresh and salt water. This can be done in small groups, as a class demonstration, or as a take-home assignment.

Materials
✓ fresh water
✓ salt water
✓ ice cube trays
✓ freezer

Procedure
1. Discuss icebergs and point out regions of the earth where icebergs can be found.

2. Have the students fill one ice cube tray with salt water and another with fresh water. Save some salt water to use later in the experiment.

3. Put both trays in the same freezer, making sure to note which one has salt water and which one has fresh water. The time it takes the water to freeze will depend on your freezer. Have a student check the water every half an hour. The fresh water will freeze first. If you leave the salt water in the freezer long enough it will also freeze.

4. Once the salt water freezes, let one of the students lick the surface of the ice cube. Have them share with the class what they taste. Compare the saltiness of the ice cube with the saltiness of the water that was reserved from filling the ice tray. Do the frozen and unfrozen forms taste the same?

5. Discuss why the fresh water froze faster and why the ice cube with salt water did not taste very salty on the top surface. Relate the findings to the use of salt on roadways in areas where the temperature drops below freezing in the winter.

6. Let one of the salt water ice cubes melt in a container after the salt on the surface has been removed. After the ice cubes melt, let one of the students taste the water. Is it as salty as the original salt water? What does this tell you about icebergs and what they are made of?

3.5 Floating Icebergs

Overview
In this experiment students will investigate water density and learn how icebergs float.

Materials
✓ water
✓ salt
✓ ice cubes (fresh water)
✓ clear glasses
✓ "Floating Icebergs" worksheet

Procedure
1. Make a batch of salt water and fill half of the clear glasses. Label them. Fill the other glasses with fresh water.

2. Have students speculate what will happen if ice cubes (miniature icebergs) are floated in fresh water and salt water. Will there be any differences?

3. Give each group two glasses, one with salt water and one with fresh water as well as two ice cubes (the ice cubes should be very close to the same size).

4. Have the students place an ice cube in each of the glasses of water and observe how much of the ice is above and below the surface of each glass. Have them draw

what they see on the worksheet and answer the questions.

5. Discuss information about icebergs as presented in the background information.

If You Live by the Ocean

Collect water from several different locations at your local beach, such as the open ocean, near a river mouth, and inside a tide pool at low tide. Evaporate an equal amount of each sample and observe the residue that is left once all the water has evaporated. You can also use equal volumes of the waters to compare density to see if there are any differences in the amount of salt in each of these types of water.

Follow-Up Questions/Activities

- What do you think happens to fresh, river water when it enters the sea?
- What would happen to the oceans if the earth's temperature rose due to global warming?
- Take two different amounts of water and put them in the freezer. Check them every half an hour until one is frozen. How does the volume or depth of water affect its freezing rate? How is this demonstrated in the real environment?
- What happens to the salinity in a tide pool on a hot day? How might this affect the plants and animals that live there?
- What might happen to the water in the world's oceans if icebergs and glaciers melted due to global warming?

Water Density

Name _____

1. **Question** - I wonder _____

_____

2. **Hypothesis** - I predict _____

_____

_____

3. **Procedure** - This is what we did _____

_____

_____

_____

_____

_____

4. **Results** - This is what happened _____

_____

_____

_____

_____

5. **Conclusion** - This showed me that _____

_____

_____

_____

Floating Icebergs

Name_____

The Experiment

Draw what happened during the experiment.

Observations

What I observed_____

_____

_____

_____

Explanation - Why do icebergs float?

Given that icebergs are fresh water, like ice cubes, what does this experiment show you about icebergs floating in sea water?_____

_____

_____

_____

Fish and Sharks

Animals with Fins and Scales

Background Information
Where Do You Find Fish?

When we think of ocean animals, fish come to mind. You can find fish in almost every body of water in the world, including oceans, lakes, rivers, streams and estuaries. The thousands of different fish species that inhabit the earth are all built for different lifestyles and environments. Some are adapted to live in the very cold water found in frozen lakes and at the bottom of the ocean. Some can live in fast-moving currents near the seashore and in rivers, and others live in complete darkness in caves and at the bottom of ocean trenches. Some are adapted for swimming fast and others for staying in one place. For almost every type of environment and lifestyle, there is a fish that is well adapted.

Characteristics of Fish

There are many differences among all the different species of fish, but there are also many similarities. Fish come in many shapes and sizes. They can be long and skinny, or shaped like a box. The largest fish is the whale shark, which is almost 18 meters in length; and the smallest fish fry measures only a few millimeters long.

All fish are vertebrates, or animals with backbones. Sharks, unlike many other fish, have bones that are made of soft cartilage, like the material in the external part of humans' ears. All fish have a mouth and nostrils, though they only use their noses to smell, not for breathing like humans.

All fish get oxygen from the water through their gills. As water passes through the fish's mouth, it is pushed over the gills, which capture the small amounts of oxygen that is in the water. Bony fish have gill covers called operculum that protect their gills. Most fish have eyes, though some fish that spend their lives in complete darkness do not. Fish also have scales that cover their body.

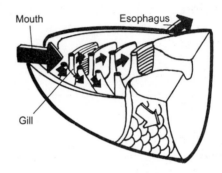

Most fish have three sets of major fins – the dorsal fin which is on their back, the caudal fin, which is also known as their tail, and pectoral fins along their sides. Many fish also have a pelvic fin and an anal fin on their undersides. Fish use these fins in different ways, some for steering, and others for moving through the water. When it comes to fins, sometimes having no fins at all helps fish like eels hide in caves. And fast swimming fish like a tuna or swordfish need a large deeply forked tail fin to keep them moving. Some fish, like the flying fish, have large pectoral fins that they use for movement, in and out of the water.

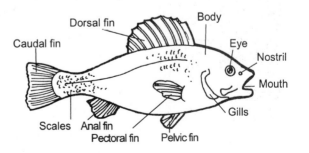

Many of the differences that we see in fish are due to their amazing ability to adapt to their environment. A fish's shape, color, mouth, and fins all can help the fish blend in to its habitat or can give it the ability to survive. When we look at body shape, a torpedo-shaped fish is designed for fast movement, a round or disc-shaped fish is designed for small, slow movements, and a flat-bottomed fish is designed for sitting on the sea floor or on a hard surface.

The color of a fish can also tell you a lot about its lifestyle. Fish that spend most of their lives swimming in the open ocean are dark colored on top and light colored on bottom; this is called counter shading. Fish that live in colorful places like a coral reef are brightly colored, and fish that are poisonous also display their defense in bright color, like the lion fish and many box fish. Many other fish match their color to their surroundings, such as the kelp fish. Flat fish like halibut can actually change colors as their environment changes.

Fish eat many different types of food. While some suck up tiny plankton, others munch on algae, and large fish even eat other smaller fish. The mouth on a fish can tell you what it eats. Fish that have teeth usually eat other fish or animals, while fish that have their mouths pointing down or on the underside of their head find their food in the sediment. A long, small mouth helps fish like the butterfly fish find food in cracks and crevices, and the beak-like mouth of the parrot fish helps it scrape algae off rocks.

Sharks

Sharks are also fish. Sharks belong to a larger group of fish that includes sharks, rays and skates. All these fish have soft cartilage bones instead of hard calcium carbonate bones like bony fish and humans. Humans have soft cartilage in our bodies also; we can feel it in the tip of our nose and in the outer part of our ears.

Sharks also have no protective covering over their gills like bony fish do. Instead of this operculum, they simply have slits in the side of their head for each gill. Shark's fins are solid, unlike bony fish, and their skin is covered with a different type of scale.

Sharks are well known for their ferocious teeth. Sharks grow their teeth in rows, and whenever one falls out (which happens very often) a new one takes its place. One shark can go through thousands of teeth in one lifetime. Other fish do not have the same type of teeth.

While many people think that sharks must continually swim to stay alive. This is only true for some sharks. Other sharks, like the nurse shark, horn shark and swell shark, spend much of their time resting on the bottom of the ocean. In the kelp forest it is common to find a variety of small sharks such as horn sharks, swell sharks, leopard sharks, bat rays, sting rays and guitar fish (a type of skate).

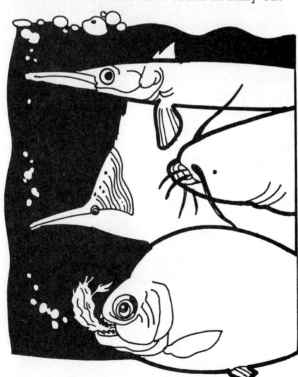

Reproduction

All fish reproduce in some fashion. Most fish lay eggs, which then turn into small fry and then into juvenile fish, and eventually grow into adult fish. Some fish lay their eggs in plants or along rocks so that they will be protected, and then the adult swims away. Other fish keep a sharp eye on their eggs until they hatch. There are even some fish that keep their eggs in their mouth. They don't eat them, but use their tongue to keep water flowing over the fragile eggs.

Some fish are internal producers, which means that while they produce eggs, the eggs never leave the mother's body, and when the fry hatch, they swim out of the mother's body, much like live birth. There are even a few sharks, like the hammerhead shark, that actually have their babies attached to the mother by umbilical cords, just like in humans.

Chapter Concepts

The main focus of this chapter is the common features and the differences among fish and sharks. The concepts presented in each lesson are:

4.1 - Breathing rates of fish

4.2 - Important features of a fish and their functions

4.3 - Relating a fish's shape to its ability to swim fast

4.4 - Adaptations required to live in a given marine environment

4.5 - Life cycles of a fish

4.6 - Comparison of scales of fish and sharks

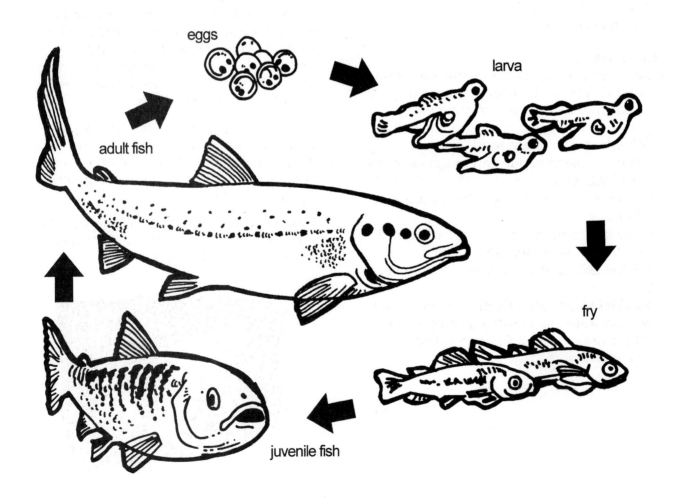

eggs

larva

adult fish

fry

juvenile fish

Fishes and Sharks

Activities

4.1 Fish Breathing

Overview

This experiment is designed for the students to monitor the breathing of a fish and determine whether the temperature of the water affects the rate of breathing. This activity is best done in four small groups. If you have more than one fish in your tank, make sure that all groups use the same fish.

Materials

- ✓ fish in an aquarium
- ✓ clock
- ✓ dark cover for tank
- ✓ warm water

Procedure

1. Refer to the background information about how fish breathe by swallowing small amounts of water and extracting the oxygen. Share this information with students. Other facts you might want to add are:
   • Water is made of one part oxygen and two parts hydrogen.
   • Humans take about 20 to 24 breaths a minute.
   • The breathing rate of fish varies from 12 to 150 breaths per minute.
   • Some fish need more oxygen than other fish.
   • Colder water can hold more oxygen than warmer water, and swiftly flowing water (like a stream) can hold more oxygen than still water.

2. Have one group of students count how many times the fish opens its mouth or moves its gills in 30 seconds. Every time the fish opens its mouth, it is breathing by taking water over its gills. Record this number on the board.

3. Next, cover the tank with a dark cover for half an hour. This simulates night for the fish. After half an hour, have the next group of students count the number of times the fish opens its mouth in 30 seconds. Record this number.

4. Have the third group of students wait at least 15 minutes with the cover off the tank before beginning their trial. Add a few cups of warm (not boiling) water to the tank (the larger the tank, the more you will need to add). All you want to do is raise the temperature of the water a few degrees. Again have the students count how many breaths the fish takes in 30 seconds.

5. Once the temperature of the tank has returned to normal (about half an hour), have the last group of students count the number of breaths in 30 seconds. See if this count is equal to your first count.

6. Discuss the results of the experiment. Ask students to speculate where fish that need more oxygen to survive might live.

4.2 Getting to Know a Fish

Overview
In this activity students will be able to show their knowledge of the parts of the fish. This can be used as a learning tool, a review, or an assessment tool.

Materials
- ✓ "Getting to Know a Fish" worksheet
- ✓ pencils
- ✓ and colored pencils (optional)

Procedure
1. Discuss the different parts of a fish and the functions of each part.

2. Give each student a copy of the worksheet and have them fill in the names of the parts of the fish and connect each name to its function.

4.3 Fast Fish — Slow Fish

Overview
In this activity students will look at the shape of a fish and determine if it is a fast or slow swimmer.

Materials
- ✓ "Fish Shapes" worksheet
- ✓ pencils

Procedure
1. Discuss basic information about how fish move through water. Include facts like:
   - Fish (with only a few exceptions) swim by wiggling their bodies and tails, much like a snake on land.
   - Many fish have bodies with streamlined shapes and smooth surfaces.
   - The torpedo shape is best for letting water flow past and allowing an object (or organism) to move through the water.

- Fish have different body shapes and some of these are better suited for fast swimming than others.
- Some fish, like the sailfish, can swim very fast (60 m.p.h. or 90 k.p.h.), while others, like the trunk fish, swim very slowly.

2. Fill a sink or tub full of water. Give students two balloons, one elongated and one shaped like a sphere. Have them move the balloons through the water and see which one meets with the most resistence.

3. Give each student a copy of the worksheet. Ask them to think about which moves faster, a torpedo or a balloon. Have students rate the fish from fastest (1) to slowest (6). It is not so important that they get the fish numbered exactly correctly as that they are able to distinguish between the fish that are fast swimmers and those that are slow swimmers and be able to explain how body shape relates to swimming speed.

4. Ask students to research the following fish and report how their body shapes relate to their abilities to move through water: sailfish, trunk fish, seahorse, sting ray, puffer fish, stone fish, barracuda,

4.4 Adaptations

Overview
In this activity your students will use their imaginations to invent a fish and will then place their fish in an environment and tell what adaptations the fish would have to make to survive in this environment.

Materials
- ✓ various craft or drawing materials

Procedure
1. Discuss some of the differences among fish – shape, color, mouth, size, and coloring – and how these differences enable them to live in a particular environment.

2. Assign half the class to invent a fish that is fast moving. Assign the other half of the class to invent a fish that is slow moving. Also give them a habitat that their fish needs to live in, such as a deep-sea trench, sandy bottom, coral reef, rocky shore, or the open sea. Have them think of different ways that their fish would have to adapt to live in this environment.

3. Students should then invent a fish that is adapted to their assigned habitat. They should be able to describe how their animal gets its food, what it might eat, how it keeps from being eaten, and what adaptations it has for movement, camouflage, defense, etc.

4.5 Life Cycle of a Fish

Overview
This lesson is a discussion of the different stages in a fish's life cycle.

Materials
✓ board and chalk
  or paper and pencils
✓ pencils

Procedure
1. Discuss the stages in a fish's life – egg, larva, fry, juvenile fish, adult fish. Share some of these interesting facts:
   • Guppies give birth to 20-70 offspring.
   • Tetras give birth to 100-150 offspring.
   • Clown barbs give birth to as many as 3,000 offspring.
   • Haddock lay about 250,000 eggs, halibut lay about 3 million eggs, and turbots lay about 9 million eggs.
   • Not all eggs hatch and many fish die young.
   • Some fish complete their entire life cycle in a year and then die.
   • Most fish live longer than a year, and some, like carp, live for 50 years or more.

   • Fish that have internal eggs have a better survival rate than fish that lay eggs.

2. Draw five boxes on the board in a circular pattern and connect them with arrows. Fill in the five stages of fish (see diagram on page 26). Or have students draw the circular diagram and fill in the five stages.

4.6 Scales

Overview
In this activity students will use their observation skills to study the differences between fish and shark scales. This lesson is presented both in this book and in the third book of this series. Ask students to do only as much as is appropriate for their age and maturation.

Materials
✓ fish and shark skin
✓ microscopes or magnifying glasses
✓ "Scales" worksheet

Procedure
1. Get a whole or piece of a fish and a piece of a shark from your local fish market. Make sure that both pieces have some skin on them. It is easy for fish scales to fall off, so a whole, small fish is better than a piece of fish.

2. Take the skin off the fish and shark. Give pieces of each to the students to examine under a microscope or magnifying glass. Have them complete the worksheet independently or in groups as they examine the two types of scales.

3. Share some of this information with students:
   - Most fish need scales to protect their delicate skin.
   - There are many different shapes and sizes of scales. The tarpon has scales that are 2 inches (50 mm.) across, and the mahseer has scales as large as a man's hands.
   - Sharks have scales that are like little teeth. They are called denticles.
   - Bony fish have scales that overlap. They are called cycloid scales.

If You Live by the Ocean

If you live by the ocean, a trip to your local marina can be very educational. You could arrange a trip aboard a fishing boat so the students could learn more about the commercial fishing industry. Also a trip to your local tide pool can give you the opportunity to see young fish in a protected environment. For a tide pool trip make sure to plan your outing during a low tide in order to be able to access the tide pool.

Follow-up Questions

- How do different fish adapt to their environment? What adaptations would enable a fish to live in the bright coral reef, a rocky area, or in the dark ocean depths?
- Show pictures of fish or sharks from books and ask students to guess if they are fast or slow swimmers, if they live on the sea floor or swim around in the water. Ask if there is anything else they can guess about the fish's life by looking at its body.
- What are some differences between fish and sharks?

Getting to Know a Fish

Name _____

Matching - Connect each body part with the phrase that describes its location on the fish's body or its function.

a. eye   ____ protects the fish's delicate skin

b. dorsal fin   ____ detects "odors" in the water

c. scales   ____ a fin on the underside that helps stabilize
                                   the fish in the water

d. nostril   ____ helps the fish see

e. pectoral fin   ____ used to eat and to swallow water

f. caudal fin   ____ another name for the tail fin

g. mouth   ____ fin on the back of the fish

h. pelvic fin   ____ collects oxygen out of the water

i. teeth   ____ this fin, along with the pelvic fin, helps
                                   stabilize the fish

j. anal fin   ____ fish use these to bite their food

k. gills   ____ fin near the operculum that helps fish steer
                                   when they swim

Label the Fish - Write the letters in the boxes to identify the body
                       parts of the fish.

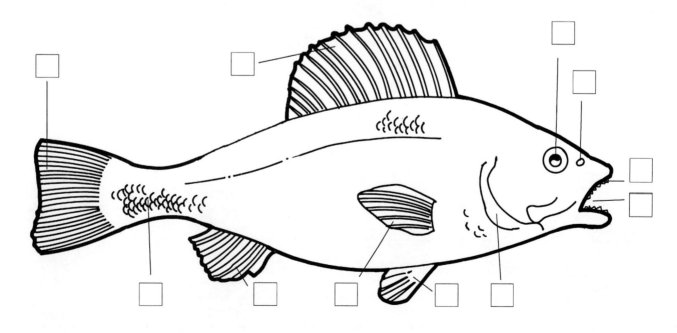

Fish Shapes

Name_____

Study the body shapes of these fish. Then put the fish in order from the fastest (1) to the slowest (6).

_____ frog fish

_____ halibut

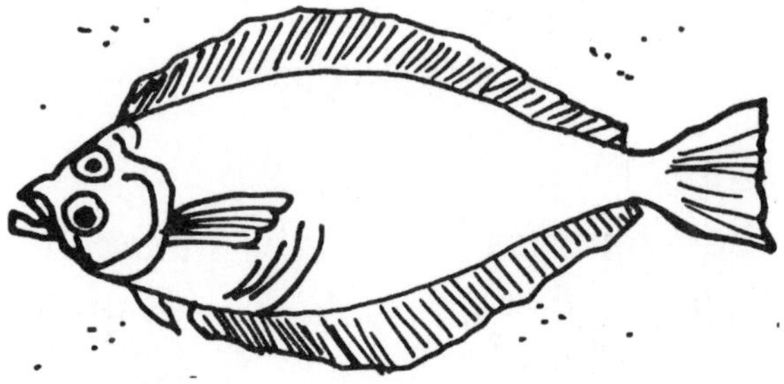

_____ tuna

_____ puffer fish

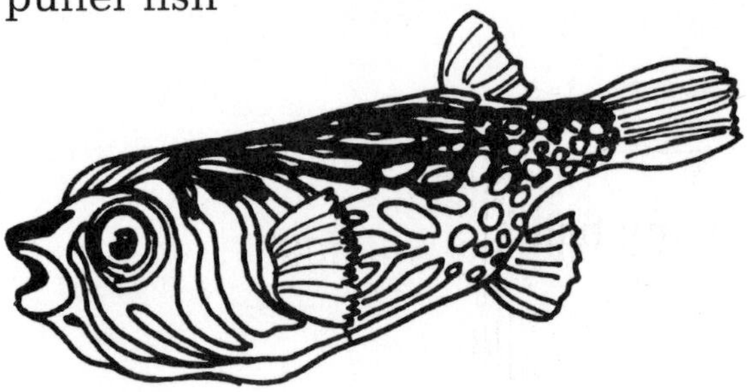

_____ whale shark

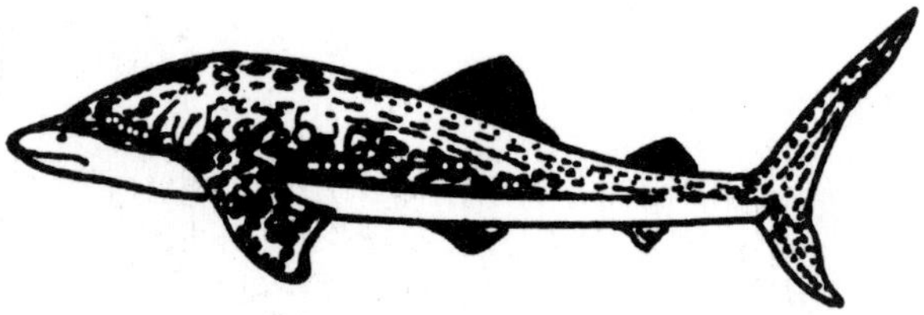

_____ blue shark

1. What do the fast fish have in common? _____

_____

2. What do the slow fish have in common? _____

_____

3. What adaptations do slower fish have that compensate for their
lack of speed? _____

_____

Scales

Name _____

1. Look at the skin of a shark and of a bony fish. Draw pictures of the two types of scales you see on the two fish.

[shark box] [bony fish box]

       shark   bony fish

2. Describe what each type of scale looks like.

    shark - _____

    _____

    bony fish - _____

    _____

3. Describe how the skin of each of these fish feels.

    shark - _____

    _____

    bony fish - _____

    _____

Marine Mammals

Splashing, Spouting Animals

Background Information

Common Traits

Whales, dolphins, seals, sea lions, sea otters, walruses and polar bears are all marine mammals. Mammals are a group of vertebrates (animals with backbones) that share common traits. These traits are:

- All mammals are warm blooded.
- Almost all mammals bear live young (the platypus lays eggs).
- All mammals nurse their young.
- All mammals breathe air through their lungs.
- Most mammals have hair (in some marine mammals hair is lost or drastically reduced in adult forms).

There are many types of mammals in the world, and most of them live on land. Other mammals besides marine mammals include cats, dogs, elephants, pigs, cows, monkeys, deer, mice, bears, and humans. What makes marine mammals different from other mammals is that they spend a majority of their lives (if not all of their lives) in the water.

Marine mammals are found in all oceans of the world and in a few rivers. While all marine mammals live in the water, they all must come to the surface to breathe. How long they can hold their breath varies from species to species, though some can hold their breath for as long as two hours, allowing them to dive deep into the ocean. Since all mammals are warm-blooded, they must keep a constant body temperature. Many marine mammals insulate themselves against the cold ocean water by growing a thick layer of blubber, while others use fur.

Variations

Though we often think of all marine mammals as being the same, there are wide variations among this group. Some, like dolphins, are built for swimming fast and catching fish with their sharp teeth, while others, like manatees, are large and slow moving and prefer to munch on plants or filter their food out of the water. Marine mammals also come in many sizes. The largest animal ever to live on the earth is a blue whale, which is as long as three school buses end to end (100 feet). Other smaller marine mammals are the size of a dog. In the following activities you will have the opportunity to learn more about some of these creatures.

Chapter Contents

This chapter introduces students to marine mammals and gives them an appreciation for how these animals are adapted to live in the ocean. The concepts presented in each lesson are:

5.1 - Characteristics of different mammals

5.2 - Size comparison of four different whales

5.3 - Demonstration of echolocation

5.4 - Incorporation of research and creative writing about a specific marine mammal

5.5 - Mind map of specific facts about some marine mammals

5.6 - Review of characteristics of marine mammals

5.7 - Review of information about marine mammals.

Marine Mammals

Activities

5.1 Marine Mammals Picture Cards

Materials

Pages 44 - 53 contain information about specific marine mammals and drawings of the animals. Cards marked **KF** are animals that live in the kelp forest. There are several different ways that you can use these cards.

Procedure

- Enlarge the pictures and put them on a bulletin board. Put a map of the world in the center of the display. Use strings to show where each animal can be found.
- Have students look up the animals in a reference book and add information to what is already provided.
- Give groups of students a set of the marine mammal cards. Read a statement from one of the cards and then say, "Who am I?" Have students hold up the card with the correct animal. You may need to give a few hints before they guess the animal.
- Introduce individual marine mammals and make a chart that shows their common characteristics.
- Make a chart or poster that has a picture of the animal and interesting facts.
- Make a map showing the animal's habitat or migration.
- Make a food chain that includes each animal.
- Use the pictures to design T-shirts or posters.
- Have students design original games (board, computer or quiz) that incorporate information about the animals.
- Have students select an animal and design a web page for that animal.

5.2 How Big Are Whales?

Overview

Students are often very interested in how big whales are. In this activity students will have the opportunity to create graphs that compare the weights and lengths of several whales.

Materials

- ✓ "How Big are Whales?" worksheet
- ✓ "How Heavy Are Whales?" worksheet
- ✓ colored pencils

Procedure

1. Discuss the different kinds of whales and the fact that they vary in size, appearance and geographical range. Point out that whales are the largest mammals on earth. They range in size from small whales like the narwhale (15 ft or 5 m) to the blue whale (about 100 ft or 30 m). Most whales do not, however, exceed 30 feet (10 m). Ask students to speculate about how many humans it would take to equal the length or weight of one whale.

2. Pass out the worksheet. Have the students use the information in the following table to create a bar graph of the whales' lengths. After they have graphed the lengths of the four whales have them graph either their heights (in meters) or the length of some other marine mammal or fish. Then have them color each bar a different color.

3. Once they are done with the first graph, pass out the second worksheet and have them graph the whales' weights.

blue whale – 30 m - 76,000 kg
sperm whale – 18 m - 32,000 kg
humpback whale – 15 m - 30,000 kg
gray whale – 12 m - 18,000 kg

statistics for other whales
right whale - 15 m - 54,000 kg
orca (killer whale) - 9 m - 5,000 kg
beluga whale - 5 m - 1,500 kg
sperm whale - 18 m - 40,000 kg
fin whale - 23 m - 59,000 kg

Extension

Give students math problems using the statistics for whales. Here are four samples:

1. How much longer is a blue whale than a humpback whale?

2. What two whales could you line up to equal the length of one blue whale?

3. About how many gray whales would it take to equal the weight of a sperm whale? a blue whale?

4. How much heavier is a sperm whale than a gray whale?

5.3 Echolocation Demonstration

Overview

This lesson will illustrate how whales and dolphins use echolocation to find food.

Materials

✓ blindfold

Procedure

1. Discuss echolocation. Give students the following information:

   • Dolphins, porpoises and many toothed whales use vocalizations to communicate with other mammals of their species and to locate things in the water.

   • Echolocation (sonar) is the animals' ability to send out high-pitched clicks and sense what is in front of them by the time it takes the echo to come back to them.

   • In addition to the pulsed sounds used for echolocation, dolphins also emit pure-tone sounds (whistles and chirps). It is believed that each animal has its own distinctive whistle.

2. Demonstrate echolocation by blindfolding one child and having him or her stand in the center of a circle of other children. Have the center person turn around a few times. Silently choose one person to be the "responder." The person in the center will slowly pivot and clap. When the student is facing the responder and claps, the responder will clap back. The blindfolded student must walk slowly towards the sound. The center person can stop and clap again and providing he or she is facing the responder, the responder will answer with a clap.

3. Discuss why even though dolphins and porpoises have good vision, echolocation might be helpful.

5.4 Writing About Marine Mammals

Overview

In this activity the students will write stories about their favorite marine mammals.

Materials

✓ marine mammal picture cards
✓ pencils
✓ scissors
✓ glue or tape

Procedure

1. Discuss how even fiction stories include factual information. Give examples of how authors use facts to create stories' settings and characters. Tell students that they will be writing a fictional story about a marine mammal.

2. Let the students pick one of their favorite marine mammals from the marine mammal cards.

3. Give the students plenty of time to create a story about their animal. Make sure that they include at least four facts about their animal in their story. They can use the facts

on the marine mammal cards and can do additional research if they need to.

4. After writing rough drafts and editing them, have students glue a picture of the animal on a separate piece of paper and write their corrected stories.

5.5 Marine Mammal Mind Map

Overview
In this activity students will create a mind map on marine mammals by brainstorming what they know about the animals.

Materials
✓ "Marine Mammal Mind Map" worksheet
✓ pencils

Procedure
1. Review similar characteristics of marine mammals and discuss some of their differences.

2. Give students a copy of the worksheet. Have them choose five different marine mammals and write the names in each of the bubbles. Then have them add words or phrases that describe each marine mammal.

3. You can also do this as a class project using an overhead projector or a bulletin board. Assign groups of students to each marine mammal and have them add facts or words to the bulletin board that describe each animal.

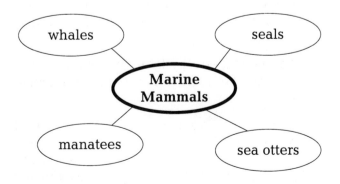

5.6 Marine Mammal Traits

Overview
In this activity students will use what they have learned about marine mammals to match each animal with words that describe it.

Materials
✓ "Marine Mammal Traits" worksheet
✓ pencils

Procedure
1. Review similarities and differences of marine mammals from previous lessons.

2. On the worksheet have students select statements that best describe each animal. There will be more than one description for each marine mammal, and some animals will share a description.

3. When finished, have them write one other characteristic or description in the space below each animal.

5.7 True, False, Opinion

Overview
This lesson will serve as a review of marine mammals by having students identify whether statements about marine mammals are true, false or opinions.

Materials
✓ "What's True About Marine Mammals?" worksheet

Procedure
1. Have students complete the "What's True About Marine Mammals" worksheet.

2. When they are finished, discuss each statement and explain why the false statements are incorrect and why the opinion statements are subjective rather than objective.

If You Live by the Ocean

If you live by the ocean you might have the opportunity to see marine mammals in their natural habitat. A field trip on a whale watching boat is an excellent way to see marine mammals of all types firsthand. Whale watching is often a seasonal outing so you should check with your local marina to book a trip during the appropriate time of the year. If a whale-watching trip is not possible, there are some places where you can see marine mammals such as seals, sea lions and dolphins from shore. Again, inquire where such a location near you may be found that is suitable for students to visit. Be sure to warn students not to approach these marine mammals. All viewing should be done from a safe distance, preferably with binoculars.

Follow-up Questions/Activities

- Have the students create a Venn diagram comparing fish and marine mammals.
- Give students a picture of a marine mammal that they have studied and ask them what adaptations they think the animal has for its environment.
- Have students learn more about endangered animals and the Marine Mammal Protection Act.
- What effect has the whaling industry had on the population of whales? What restrictions are in place? Which countries still practice whaling? What should be done about this?

How Big Are Whales?

Name_____

Make a graph that compares the lengths of four different kinds of whales. For the fifth section of the graph, show either your height or the length of some other marine mammal or fish.

length (meters)	blue whale	sperm whale	humpback whale	gray whale	
30—					
25—					
20—					
15—					
10—					
5—					

How Heavy Are Whales?

Name _____

Make a graph that compares the
weights of four different kinds of
whales and a marine mammal of
your choosing.

weight (kg.)	blue whale	sperm whale	humpback whale	gray whale	
80,000—					
60,000—					
40,000 —					
20,000—					

Marine Mammal Mind Map

Name _____

Complete this mind map by writing the names of five different marine mammals in the bubbles and adding information about these animals.

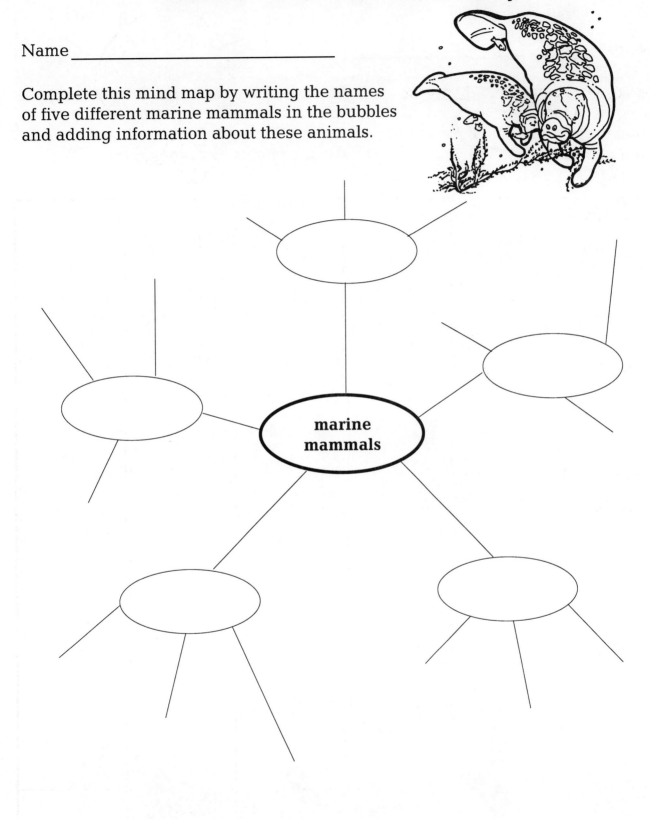

Marine Mammal Traits

Name _____

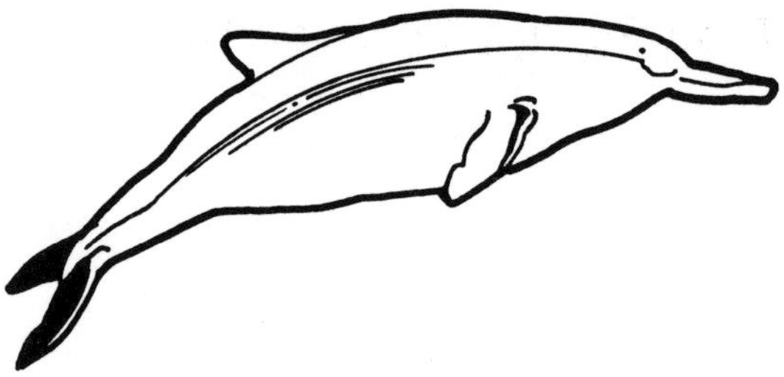

On the line by each marine mammal, write the letters of the statements that are true for that animal. You will use some of the statements more than once.

a. largest marine mammal

_____ whale

b. swims very slowly

c. lives in kelp

_____ sea otter

d. crawls on land

e. some have baleen

_____ seal

f. uses rocks as tools

g. uses echolocation

_____ dolphin

h. a member of the pinniped family

i. has blubber

_____ walrus

j. eats fish

k. breathes air

_____ manatee

l. eats plants

m. has live birth

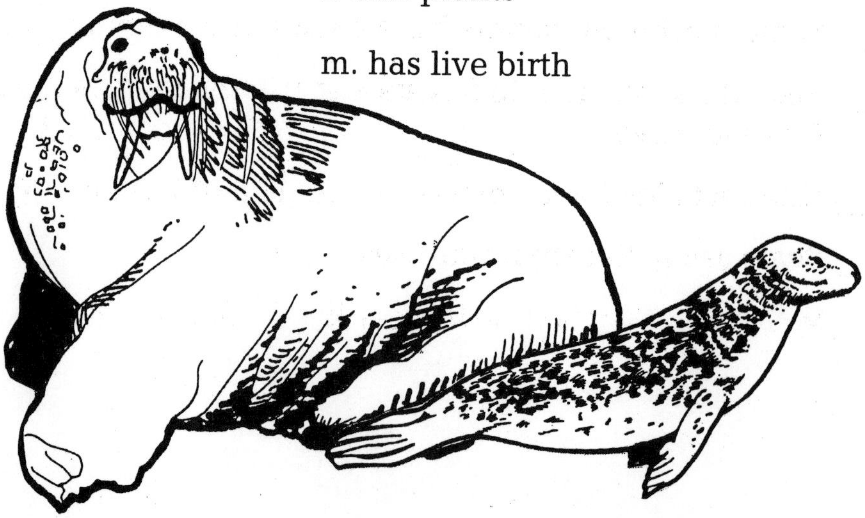

What's True About Marine Mammals?

Name_____

For each statement tell whether it is true (**T**), false (**F**), or an opinion (**O**).

1. _____ Dolphins and porpoises are toothed whales.

2. _____ Harbor seals are cute and should not be killed.

3. _____ Manatees are swift swimmers.

4. _____ Baleen whales eat very small animals called krill.

5. _____ Echolocation is used by toothed whales to express emotions.

6. _____ Marine mammals give live birth.

7. _____ Marine mammals either use thick fur or a layer of blubber to keep warm.

8. _____ The largest mammal on earth is the blue whale.

9. _____ Dolphins and porpoises are swift swimmers and can leap out of the water.

10. _____ Dolphins are the best acts at sea life parks like Sea World.

11. _____ Some marine mammals have been hunted almost to extinction.

12. _____ Sea otters live in kelp forests and use the kelp as anchors to keep from floating away.

13. _____ Killer whales (orca whales) are large and hunt by themselves.

14. _____ Seals are better than walruses.

15. _____ Walruses and polar bears only live in the cold Arctic.

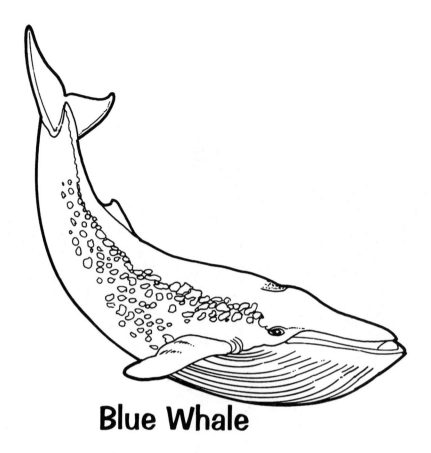

Blue Whale

The blue whale is a baleen whale, like the gray whale, humpback whale, right whale and fin whale. Instead of teeth, baleen whales have long sheets of baleen that hang from the top of their mouths. Whales use the baleen to filter small shrimp called krill out of the water. In addition to baleen, they have pleated throat grooves that expand so they can take in large amounts of water while feeding. This whale consumes approximately one ton of food at each meal.

Like many other baleen whales, blue whales feed during the summer season in the cold polar waters where food is plentiful. They spend the rest of the year traveling through all the oceans of the world. Mating occurs at the end of the winter, with a single calf being born 10 to 11 months later when the whale is in the warmer waters. Blue whales may live to be 100 years or more.

The blue whale is the largest animal to ever inhabit earth. It grows to be 30 meters long and weighs about 80,000 kilograms. It is also the loudest animal on earth. Its call is louder than a jet and can be heard hundreds of miles away. They live individually or in small groups called pods.

These gray-blue colored whales have two blowholes near the top of their heads in a large raised area and a very small dorsal fin located near the flukes (tail). They have long, thin flippers 8 feet long (2.4 m) and flukes that are 25 feet (7.6 m) wide. They have a thick layer of blubber that keeps them warm. Blue whales can submerge for 20 minutes, going to a depth of 105 meters and can swim at a speed of 20 miles per hour.

44

Orca Whale

The orca is a toothed whale like the sperm whale, narwhale, and beluga whale. Unlike the baleen whales, toothed whales have mouths full of cone-shaped teeth. Orcas have 48 sharp teeth. They have only one blowhole on the top of their head that they use for breathing. Orcas also have a triangular dorsal fin between the head and tail.

Orcas have distinctive coloration with black on the top portion of their bodies, a white patch around each eye and a white belly. Orcas, like other toothed whales, are usually smaller than baleen whales. Males can reach 30 feet (9 meters) in length and weigh more than 8,000 pounds (4,500 kilograms), while females are about half that size. Females give birth to a single calf.

The orca or killer whale is an efficient predator that eats a very diverse diet of fish, squid, marine mammals (including seals, sea lions, porpoises, and even some whales), turtles, octopuses, and birds (penguins and gulls). They hunt for larger animals in groups.

Orcas live in small, close-knit, life-long pods of from 6 to 40 whales. They are very social animals and hunt together in a very sophisticated manner. Orcas can dive to a depth of 30 meters in order to hunt and can swim as fast as 30 mph.

Orcas range from tropical to arctic oceans and both coastal and deep oceanic waters. They are found in all the world's oceans and most of the seas but are most numerous in the Arctic, the Antarctic, and areas of cold water upwellings.

Harbor Porpoise

Of all the members of the porpoise family, the harbor porpoise is the best known. Porpoises are different from dolphins in that they have rounded noses and triangular dorsal fins. Like most porpoises, the harbor porpoise is small in comparison to other marine mammals, with a body length of 1.5 to 2.0 meters and a weight of 55 kilograms. Female porpoises are usually bigger than the males. Life expectancy for this species is approximately 15 years.

Like many other porpoises, the harbor porpoise is quite shy and keeps away from boats. Because of this shy personality, they are not often observed in the wild. When observed, they are usually alone or in pairs. Occasionally they are seen in large groups, probably for migration or to take advantage of rich feeding grounds.

The harbor porpoise's diet is comprised mainly of squid and fish. These porpoises tend to prefer fishes such as herrings, mackerels, and sardines. They are able to dive very deep (over 200 meters) to get their food.

Harbor porpoises are found in the coastal waters of the North Atlantic and Northern Pacific. Their name comes from the fact that they are frequently found in bays, rivers, estuaries, and tidal channels.

Bottlenose Dolphin

Dolphins are small toothed whales, and like the orca, they have many cone-shaped teeth. Like all dolphins, the bottlenose dolphin has an elongated nose or rostrum and a curved dorsal fin. It has horizontal tail flukes that it uses for swimming. The dolphin's streamlined body makes it a swift swimmer, reaching speeds of 24 miles per hour. They are relatively small (2.3 to 3.1 meters) compared to other toothed whales like the sperm whale.

Bottlenose dolphins are found in almost all coastal areas except for the polar regions. They feed on squid and fish such as mullet, anchovies, herring, cod and menhaden.

More than any other dolphin, the bottlenose forms long-term associations with such widely different species as sea turtles, humpback whales and humans. They are social animals that live together in relatively stable units of up to 100 individuals. Like most dolphins, they use vocalizations both for locating objects (echolocation) and to communicate with other dolphins.

The bottlenose dolphin is one of the best known dolphins because it has been shown in aquariums since the 1860s. Its friendly nature and natural tendency for acrobatics has led to its common appearance in aquariums and water parks.

Females give birth to a single calf that stays very close to the mother for several months after birth. It is believed that wild bottlenose dolphins can live well into their forties.

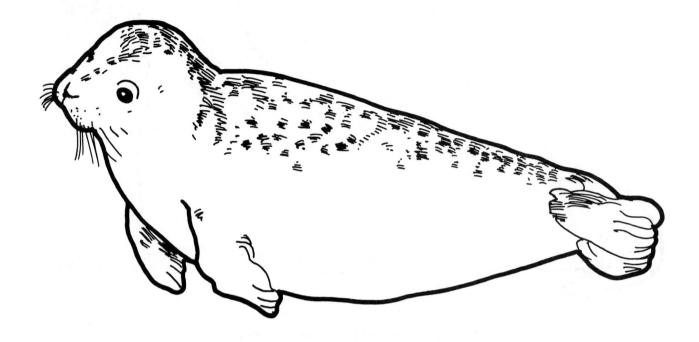

Harbor Seal

The harbor seal is the most widely distributed seal, inhabiting temperate and subarctic coastal areas on both sides of the north Atlantic and north Pacific Oceans. It is a member of the pinniped (meaning feathered foot) family.

Seals have a thick layer of blubber to help keep them warm. Harbor seals are often gregarious, hauling out on rocky shores, reefs, beaches, sand bars, piers, and glacial ice in groups to breed and rest. Small colonies of several families will occupy the same location for generations. Harbor seals tend to stay within 20 kilometers of the shore, but individual animals are occasionally found 100 kilometers or more offshore.

Harbor seals have sharp teeth. Usually they are solitary hunters that feed on a large number of species of small fish, crabs, squid and octopuses. Their greatest enemies are sharks and killer whales.

Harbor seals, like other seals, use their rear flippers for swimming and can dive as deep as 500 meters for short periods of time. Male harbor seals are much larger (1.7 meters in length and weighing 125 kilograms) than females (1.4 meters long and weighing 75 kilograms).

48

California Sea Lion

California sea lions inhabit rocky and sandy beaches of coastal islands and mainland shorelines. On land, they gather in large groups called colonies. They are found on the Pacific coast of North America from southern Canada to Mexico, as well as the Galapagos Islands. They feed on fish, octopus and squid found in these coastal waters.

The sea lion is a member of the pinniped family that includes seals and walruses. Like all sea lions, California sea lions can bend their rear flippers under their bodies to sit upright and use their long front flippers to swim. As in many seals and sea lions, males are larger (2.5 meters in length and weighing 300 kilograms) than females (2.0 meters and 100 kilograms). Both males and females have a layer of blubber to keep them warm.

California sea lions can dive as deep as 120 meters and can stay submerged for up to 20 minutes and swim at speeds up to 25 mph. California sea lions are very vocal, making barking sounds that can be heard from quite a distance.

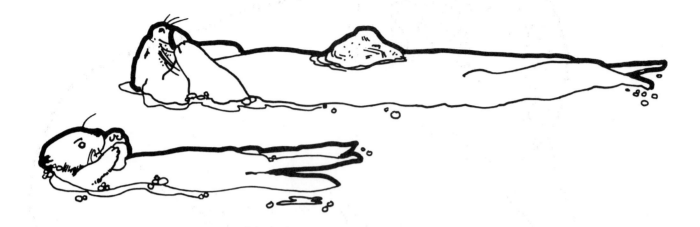

Sea Otter

Sea otters are small marine mammals that live in the kelp forests off the coasts of Japan, Alaska, Canada, Washington, Oregon and California. They are related to river otters and are part of the weasel family.

They have sleek, furry bodies and long tails. Their front forearms have stubby paws and finger-like extensions that they use to pick up food and rocks. Their short hind legs have webbed feet that are used for swimming. Instead of having a layer of blubber, they are kept warm by a layer of air that is trapped by their thick coats of fur.

They have sharp teeth and eat fish and hard shelled animals like sea urchins, abalone, crabs and clams that they find while swimming near the rocky floor of the kelp forest. In order to break open the hard shells of their food, sea otters float on their backs and use a flat rock placed on their belly as a tool to break the shells against. They consume 25 percent of their body weight in food each day.

Sea otters swim, rest, sleep and eat on their backs. They spend much of their time on top of the water wrapped in kelp to keep them from floating away or from being attacked by a passing shark or killer whale.

At one time they ranged the entire Pacific coast from Alaska to Baja, California. Hunted for their fur during the 18th and 19th century, they became almost extinct. They are gradually growing in number and reestablishing their territory.

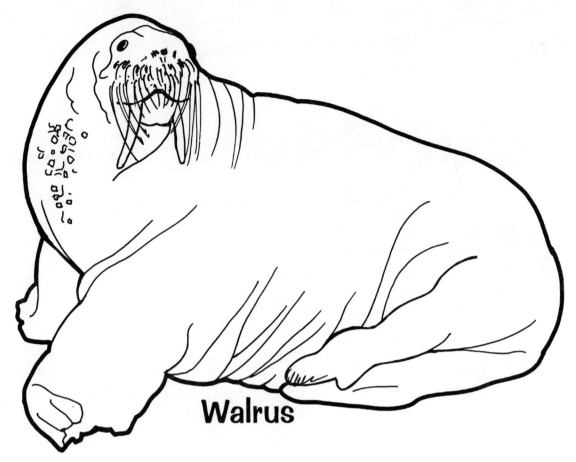

Walrus

The walrus lives in the chilly waters of the northern Atlantic and Pacific oceans. It is the largest of the pinnipeds. While the walrus is a marine mammal and lives in shallow water, it spends a lot of time out of water sleeping on ice or rocks. Colonies resting on beaches or ice floes can number as many as 100 animals. Herds of walrus tend to follow the ice line, moving south in the winter and north in the summer.

The walrus is related to seals and sea lions, but it looks very different. Walruses have two large tusks or teeth that grow out of their upper jaws. The tusks can be 3 feet (1 meter) long. With these two large tusks the walrus pulls its large body up on sheets of ice. It also has quill-like whiskers in its muzzle or cheeks. The walrus uses these long whiskers to find clams, crabs, snails and worms in the muddy bottom of the ocean.

The walrus has thick, wrinkled, nearly-hairless hide and blubber to keep itself warm. It has a bark that sounds like a dog's bark. Male walrus are about 10 feet (3 meters) in length and weigh up to 3,000 pounds (1,400 kilograms), while females are smaller.

Commercially hunted for its blubber, hide and ivory since the 16th century, the population of walruses was greatly reduced. Some types of walruses are nearly extinct, and many countries now prohibit hunting walruses.

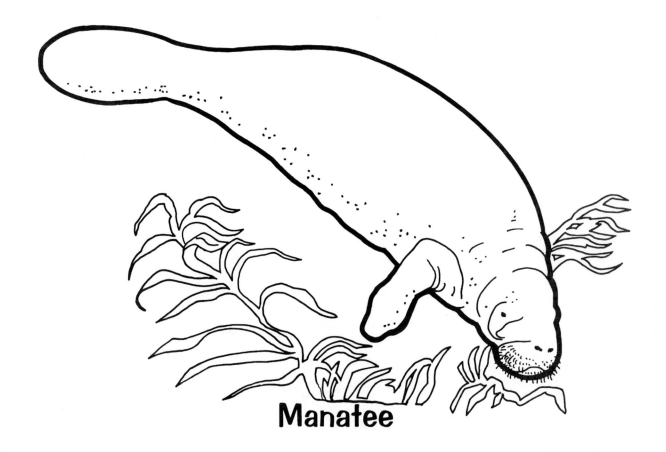

Manatee

Manatees are large, marine mammals that live in the warm, shallow coastal waters of Florida, the Gulf of Mexico, the Caribbean Sea, coastal South America, and west Africa. They are often found in bays, coastal inlets and shallow reefs. Because they have very little fat to keep them warm, they must stay in warm water. They are gentle and slow-moving and spend most of their time eating, resting and traveling. They can travel 40 to 50 miles a day.

Manatees are the only marine mammals that are plant-eaters, dining mostly on sea grasses. A manatee can eat as much as 100 pounds of underwater plants a day. An adult manatee is between 9 to 13 feet long and weighs between 1,000 and 3,000 pounds.

Manatees have two forelimbs that they use both for swimming and grabbing food. Their skin is thick and wrinkled. Unlike other marine mammals, their tails are round, powerful paddles. Like the walrus, they have whiskers around their mouth that they use for feeling the ocean floor. They do not have external ear lobes but can hear very well. They breathe through nostrils that can close tightly when they are submerged. They breathe every few minutes when they are active and only every 10 to 15 minutes when they are resting. Manatees communicate by making sounds that are like squeals or squeaks.

Since manatees are large slow-moving animals that float near the surface of the water, they are susceptible to pollution from land and being hit by fast moving boats.

Polar Bear

Polar bears are not often thought of as marine mammals, but since they spend much of their time in the cold waters of the Arctic looking for food, they are in fact marine mammals. Polar bears usually live on ice drifts but sometimes come on land.

Polar bears are the only bears that are white in color to blend in with their icy environment. Even though the polar bear looks white, its skin is black so that it can absorb heat from the sun to keep itself warm. Polar bears also have fur on the soles of their feet to help them walk on ice. Adult males are between 7 to 9 feet (200 - 300 cm) tall and weigh between 700 and 1600 pounds (320 - 730 kilograms). Female polar bears are smaller.

They are usually solitary animals, with the exception that cubs stay close to their mothers. Polar bears are fairly good swimmers and have been seen swimming 50 miles away from ice or land. Polar bears dive beneath ice sheets to look for fish and seals to eat. They can also walk long distances across ice in order to find food.

While they are omnivorous, they mainly eat seals and young walruses. During the summer they will eat vegetation along the shoreline. They are fearless and have no real enemies except humans. Because of extensive hunting, their numbers have declined.

Invertebrates

Squishy, Slippery Animals

Background Information

What Are Invertebrates?

Most of the animals on earth are invertebrates (animals without backbones). They include animals such as jellyfish, coral, sponges, worms, mussels, octopuses, limpets, sea anemones, sea slugs, barnacles, sea urchins, sand dollars, crabs, clams, snails, sea stars, ladybugs, grasshoppers, ants and spiders. Both in the number of individual animals and in the number of different species, invertebrates far outnumber vertebrates (animals with backbones), especially in the ocean. Invertebrates are the predominant life form in the kelp forest environment.

Invertebrates are found in all environments from deep-sea trenches to dry desert. They can fly through the air, walk on land, or swim in the ocean. They can be as tiny as a speck of dust or as large as a bus. Some are fast swimmers and others spend their entire life in one place. Some have thick, hard shells while others are very fragile. Some invertebrates, such as sponges, are very simple animals, with no organs, nervous system or eyes. Others, like the octopus, are quite intelligent with very complex, well-developed organs and nervous systems.

Shells or No Shells

Scientists classify organisms into groups based on their characteristics. These major groups of animals are called phyla (phylum) and they help scientists understand the relationships between all organisms. While all vertebrates are in one phylum, there are over 20 different phyla for the invertebrates that inhabit the earth. The following is an outline of the five major invertebrate phyla that inhabit the ocean.

✳ Porifera – pore-bearing animals

This group contains the simplest animals on earth, the sponges. Sponges are animals, but they look a lot like plants. Sponges are found only in the ocean, living on hard substrates. They can be large enough for a person to fit inside, but many are smaller than your hand. They have no brain, no organs, no nerves, eyes or mouths. They have holes, or pores, all over their bodies that water continually moves through. They filter microscopic organisms out of the water that they circulate through their body. Often, humans harvest sponges to use as bath products.

✳ Cnidarians – stinging animals

This group contains animals such as jellyfish, sea anemones and coral. All these animals have a jelly-like body and microscopic stinging cells called nematocysts. The cnidarians are also very simple animals. Like the porifera, they have no brain, eyes or organs. They have a diffuse net of nerves and a mouth surrounded by tentacles that opens into a sac-like gut. While sea anemones and jellyfish are very soft, corals secrete a hard structure under their tissue. Over time, the hard structures of millions of coral animals builds up into giant coral reefs.

✱ Mollusca – soft bodied animals

This group contains animals with soft bodies such as snails, slugs, octopus, squid, clams, mussels and chitons. These animals all have a soft body and a muscular foot. Mollusks also have eyes, a brain, a nervous system and organs. Some animals in this group, like clams, snails, and nautilus, also have a shell. Mollusks make their shell from a special layer of their skin; the shell keeps growing with the animal throughout its life. These animals are found both on land and in the water.

✱ Echinodermata – spiny skinned animals

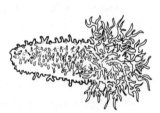

This group of animals contains animals with spiny skin such as sea urchins, sea stars, brittle stars and sea cucumbers. All these animals also have five-sided symmetry and tube feet that they use to move and hang onto rocks. While these animals are complex, they do not have eyes or a true brain. Some sea stars have eye spots on the end of each arm that sense light. Echinoderms have the ability to regenerate parts of their bodies, such as an arm, if it breaks off or is damaged by a predator. This group of invertebrates is only found in the ocean.

✱ Arthropoda – jointed legged animals

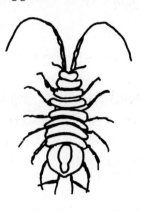

This group of invertebrates includes animals with an exoskeleton and jointed legs such as crabs, insects, spiders and shrimp. A sub-phyla of the arthropods are the crustaceans, which include only the ocean animals such as crabs, lobsters, shrimp, barnacles and krill. These animals have segmented bodies and antennae. They are complex animals with brains, eyes, nervous systems and organs. As these animals grow, they shed their exoskeleton and grow a new one. This is called molting.

Chapter Concepts

This chapter introduces students to marine invertebrates and gives them an appreciation for how these animals are adapted to live in the ocean. The concepts presented in each lesson are:

6.1 - Various activities using pictures and information

6.2 - Categorization of invertebrates

6.3 - Hatching and observing brine shrimp

6.4 - Squid dissection

6.5 - Creation of an invertebrate that incorporates adaptations for survival

Animals Without Backbones

Activities

6.1 Invertebrate Animal Picture Cards

Materials
✓ picture cards

Pages 64 - 74 contain information about specific marine invertebrate animals and drawings of the animals. The animals that have a **KF** on the page are animals that live in the kelp forest. There are several different ways that you can use these cards.

Ways to use the cards

- Use the animal cards to introduce the animals to the class. Have students share what they already know about the animals.

- Have students look up the animals in a reference book and add information to what is already provided.

- Give groups of students a set of the invertebrate animal cards. Read a statement from one of the cards and then say, "Who am I?" Have students hold up the card with the correct animal. You may need to give a few hints before they guess the animal.

- Have students design original games (board, computer or quiz) that incorporate information about the animals.

- Have students select an animal and design a web page for that animal.

- Have students select an animal and make a box of ten statements, some of which are true and some of which are false. Have them trade boxes and divide the statements into true and false piles.

- Make posters or charts that include pictures of the animals along with interesting facts.

6.2 Getting to Know Invertebrate Phyla

Overview
In this activity students will learn how scientists sort animals into different groups and what the major marine phyla of invertebrates are. **This activity should be done before the invertebrate phyla are introduced.**

Materials
✓ "Invertebrate Phyla" worksheets
✓ scissors

Procedure
1. Make several copies of the worksheets and cut apart the pictures of the marine invertebrates.

2. Give each group of students an entire set of cards and ask them to sort them into groups. Let the students use any sorting method that they want, but have them make between two and six groupings of animals.

3. After they are done sorting, have them explain their sorting methods. Introduce the five phyla.

4. Give the students the cards again after you have introduced the phyla and see if they can classify the animals into those five groups. This can be done occasionally throughout the unit to reinforce or test their knowledge.

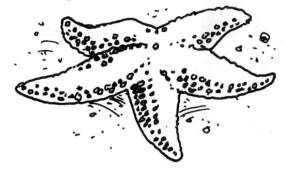

6.3 Growing Crustaceans - Sea Monkeys

Overview
One fun way to get a close up view of some marine invertebrates is to hatch sea monkeys. Sea monkeys are actually crustaceans called brine shrimp that you can buy in packets and grow in your classroom.

Materials
✓ packet of sea monkeys
✓ microscope or magnifying glass

Procedure
1. Review the phyla of Arthropoda. Discuss what this word means (*arthro* - jointed and *pod* - foot). Review also that crustaceans are a special subgroup of arthropod. Tell students that they will be growing and observing crustaceans.

2. The packets have complete instructions for hatching the tiny crustaceans. Follow the directions in your packet.

3. Have students observe the sea monkeys under magnification and do one or more of the following:
   • make drawings of the creatures every day for a week to track their development
   • write their observations
   • complete the sentence, "A sea monkey is like ___, " as many ways as possible

Sea monkeys can live for quite a while and may even live long enough to produce eggs and a new generation.

6.4 Squid Dissection

Overview
Students will dissect squids and examine their body parts. This lesson is presented both in this book and in the third book of this series. Ask students to do only as much as is appropriate for their age and maturation.

Materials
✓ 1 squid per child (or pair of children)
✓ sharp scissors
✓ newspaper
✓ plastic plates
✓ paper towels
✓ "Dissecting a Squid" worksheets

Procedure
1. Purchase whole frozen squid from your local supermarket or fish market. Make sure to give them plenty of time to defrost before the dissection. Cover the tables with newspaper and place a squid on a paper towel that is on a plastic plate. You can either give a squid to each student or have them work in pairs. For each squid you dissect you will also need a pair of scissors.

2. Start with the squid lying with its dorsal side up as in the picture on page 62. The dorsal side can be distinguished by the presence of many small purple spots, the fins are continuous with the mantle, and there is a pointed tip to the mantle near the squid's head.

3. Have students count the tentacles and arms. There should be eight short arms and two long tentacles. Have them look for suction cups. Then have them gently rub the fins. This will open the chromatophores, the pigment cells in the skin, and the skin will turn more purple.

4. Have them open up the arms and look in the center; this is where the squid's mouth is. The mouth is a beak, like that of a parrot. The beak is surrounded by a bundle of muscles called the buccal mass. Have the students gently pull out the mouth and buccal mass.

5. Next have students turn the squid over so the dorsal side is down. Have them look at the eyes. Extending from under the mantle towards the eyes is the siphon. It is a hollow tube that the squid uses to squirt water for jet propulsion. Have students lift up the edge of the mantle and notice that it is also a tube, like a sock.

6. Now have the students carefully use their scissors to cut the mantle from the siphon to the tip. To make sure that none of the organs get damaged, it is best to hold up the mantle while it is being cut. Once that cut is made, the mantle can be opened up and the organs will be exposed.

7. Using the illustration on page 63, help the students to find the organs, such as the gills. If you have a squid that is a female, there will be two predominant white cylindrical sacks extending from the point of the mantel into the body cavity. These are the ovaries. It is best to cut them out to better view the organs.

8. Squid have three hearts, one at the top of each gill and one large one in between the other two. Have the students find these.

9. Squid also have ink sacs like octopus. The ink sac is a small black/silver organ near the center of the squid. Have the students carefully cut it out and place it on the edge of their paper towel.

10. Once the students have identified all the major organs of the squid, have them take out one of the lenses of the squid's eye. It is a hard round ball.

11. Now have the students fold the tentacles and head up into the mantle cavity. This will expose the bottom surface of the mantle. If they run their finger along the edge they will feel a hard ridge. This is the pen, the vestigial shell of the squid. Have the students pull it out. It will look like a clear piece of plastic. They can use this to dip in the ink sac and write their name in squid ink on their paper towel.

12. Once they are done, have the students throw away their squid on its paper towel and wash the plastic plate (or dispose of it) and wash off their scissors. You will want to make sure that the garbage gets taken out so that your classroom will not smell bad and attract insects.

6.6 Make an Invertebrate

Overview
This lesson will serve as a fun review of invertebrates and what kinds of adaptations they have that allow them to survive.

Materials
- ✓ squares of gelatin
- ✓ waxed paper
- ✓ various craft materials, paper tubes
- ✓ glue, tape

Procedure
1. Make a batch of gelatin thick enough to be cut into squares. Make one small square for each child.

2. Review what you have learned about invertebrates, in particular different ways that invertebrates move, catch food, and defend themselves from prey.

3. Give each child a square of gelatin on a piece of waxed paper. Challenge them to make adaptations for their "invertebrate animals" that will allow the animals to defend themselves, move away from predators and/or catch food. They may not be able to accomplish all of these objectives, but they should give their invertebrates at least one adaptation that will allow it to survive.

4. When finished, share invertebrate creations and let students explain their adaptations.

If You Live by the Ocean

If you live by the ocean, you may have the opportunity to visit a tide pool first hand and look for marine invertebrates. Most of the tide pool environment is covered with marine invertebrates. You can find snails, sea stars, limpets, crabs, sea anemones, and maybe even an octopus. Many of the invertebrates are small and well-camouflaged, so you will have to look closely. Lift up seaweed or rocks carefully to look for hidden invertebrates. But be careful where you walk, for many invertebrates will be right underfoot. Before you go, make sure to pick a location that allows safe entry into the tide pool area; not all tide pools are easily accessible or safe for students. Also make sure to check your local tide charts to pick a time when the tide is low. If you go at high tide, the students will not be able to approach the tide pool at all. It is best for students to always wear shoes in tide pools. And make sure to tell students that all the creatures are alive and that they must be very careful about handling and walking around these fragile creatures. If an animal is attached to a rock, tearing it off will often kill it, so it is best to gently touch animals where they are. Also be aware that in most states it is illegal to take any animals from the tide pool without the proper permits (these are different from fishing permits).

Follow-Up Questions/Activities

- Have the students draw a picture of their favorite invertebrate and tell how it is adapted to survive in its environment.
- List the similarities and differences between marine invertebrates and fish.
- Many invertebrates are good to eat. Have a class party where the students can taste many marine invertebrates such as clams, squid, and shrimp.
- If you have not already made a kelp forest mural as part of the unit on ecosystems, the invertebrate unit is an excellent time to do so. Make a mural of a kelp forest on a bulletin board. You can have the top of the board be the surface of the water and the bottom of the board or the floor be the ocean floor. Make rocks and plenty of kelp, each with a holdfast. Have the students color and cut out invertebrate animals and fish that can be found in a kelp forest and place them in the mural. Include sea snails, sea urchins, sea anemones, abalone, octopus, lobster, squid, crab, sea star, jellyfish, tube worms, and brittle stars.
- Some invertebrates such as abalone and some varieties of clams are nearly extinct. Find out what is being done to preserve this resource.
- Choose an invertebrate. What can you add to it or how can you change it to make it better able to survive?
- Choose an invertebrate. Draw a food chain that includes it, its prey and its predators.
- Get a supply of shells from scientific supply sources or from students' collections. Have students group them. Discuss their similarities and differences.

Invertebrate Phyla

 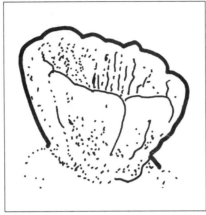 

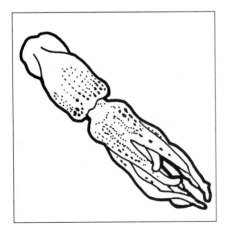  

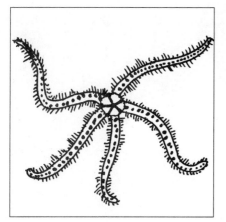

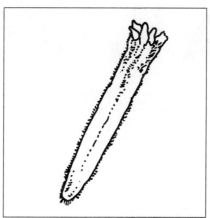

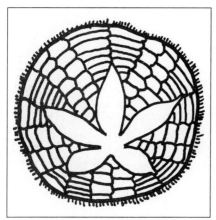

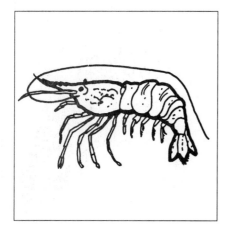

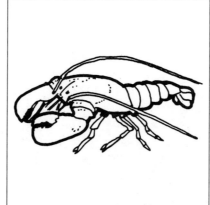

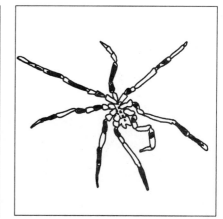

Dissecting a Squid

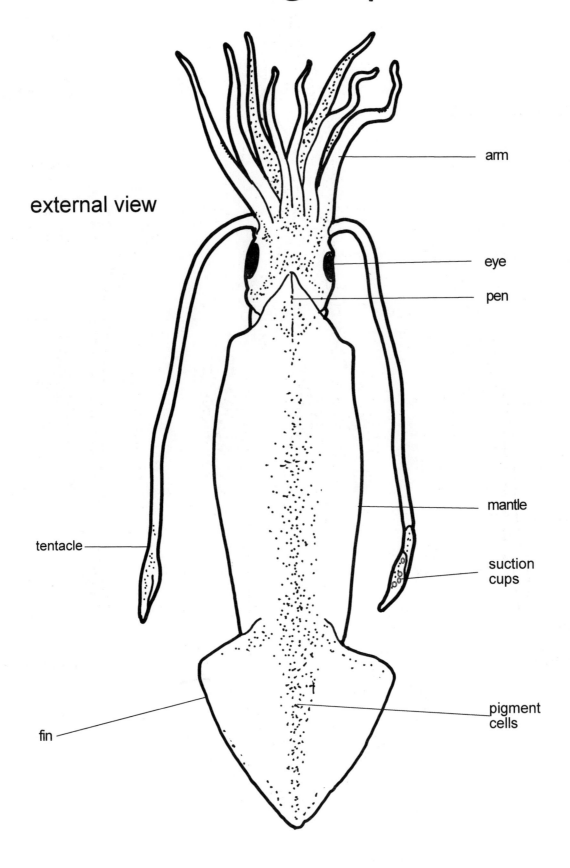

external view

arm

eye

pen

mantle

tentacle

suction
cups

fin

pigment
cells

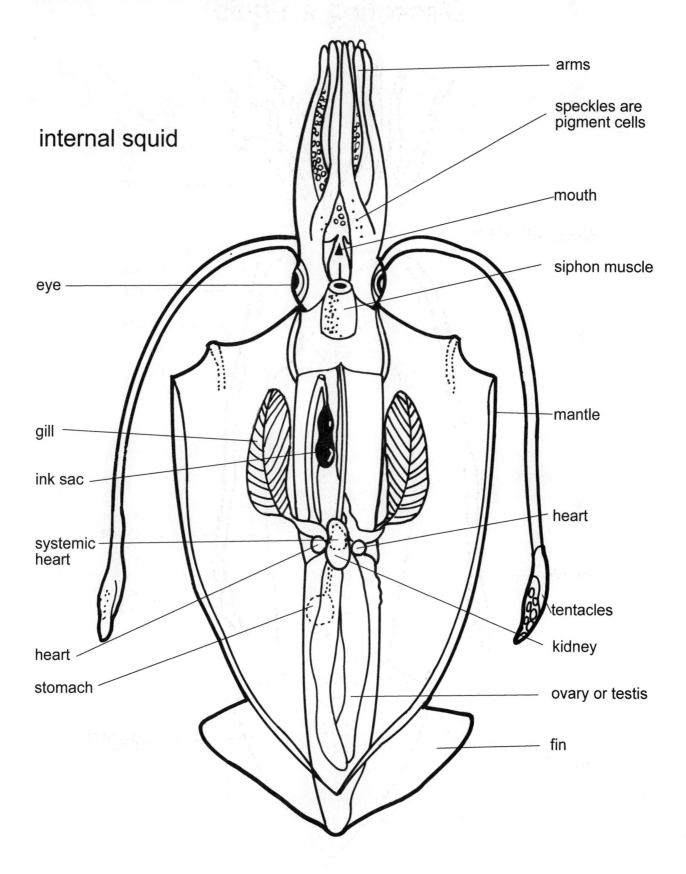

internal squid

arms

speckles are
pigment cells

mouth

siphon muscle

eye

mantle

gill

ink sac

heart

systemic
heart

tentacles

kidney

heart

stomach

ovary or testis

fin

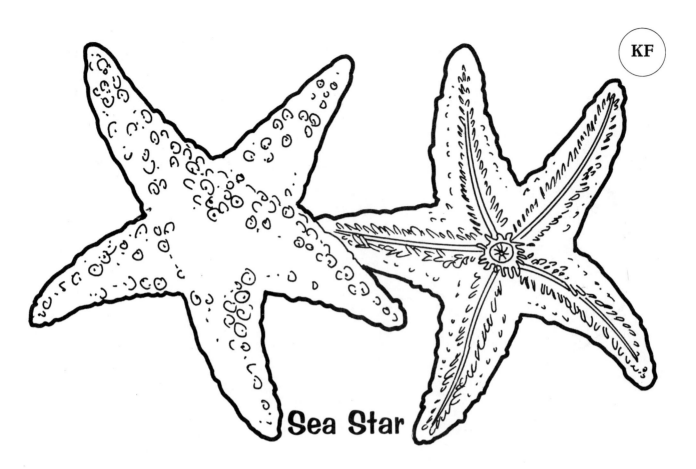

Sea Star

The sea star is one of the most familiar marine invertebrates. There are many different types of sea stars, but most have five arms that radiate from a central disk. While most sea stars have five arms, some have six, and a few have as many as 25. Each arm has rows of tiny tube feet on the underside. These tube feet have lots of powerful suction cups that help the sea star cling to rocks while the waves crash around it.

Sea stars are members of a group of animals called echinoderms. Echinoderm means "spiny skin." Sea stars have small spines all over their bodies. Other relatives of the sea star are sea urchins, sand dollars and sea cucumbers.

Sea stars can be found in many coastal areas. They are scavengers, eating a variety of different things (snails, urchins, limpets, sponges, and sea anemones). The sea star's favorite food is mussels. It pulls the two shells of the mussel apart and sticks its stomach into the shell to eat the mussel. Its predators are birds, sea otters, and humans (who collect them but do not eat them).

If a sea star loses an arm, it can regrow it; and if it is cut in half, each half can regrow the missing part. The sea star has no brain and no true eyes, but it has light-sensitive spots on the end of each arm.

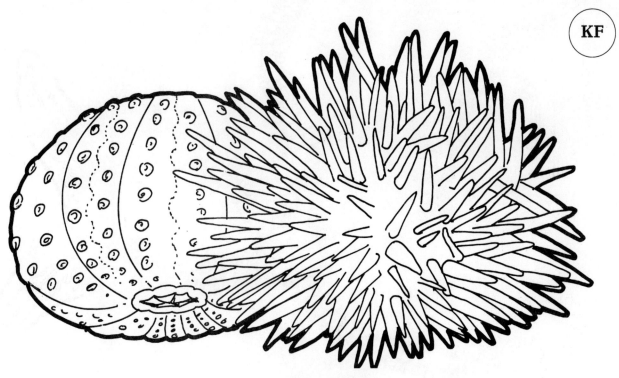

Sea Urchin

The sea urchin is an echinoderm like the sea star. It lives in tide pools, on the rocky sea floor and in kelp forests. The sea urchin is shaped like a ball, but with thousands of red or purple spines all over its body. The spines are often poisonous.

Sea urchins are usually about 4 inches in diameter, but red sea urchins are about 7 inches (18 centimeters) in diameter.

Like a sea star, the sea urchin has tube feet, but its feet are all over its body, not just on the bottom. The sea urchin uses its tube feet to cling to rocks, to move, and to catch drifting algae for food.

Like the sea star, the sea urchin has a claw-like mouth on the bottom of its body. It has five teeth. It uses these teeth to scrape algae off the rocks and kelp and to bite pieces of algae. A large group of sea urchins can destroy a kelp forest by eating it. Besides algae, sea urchins also dine on decaying matter, kelp, dead fish, sponges, mussels and barnacles.

Since the sea urchin has long spines, not many other animals like to eat it. One of its enemies is the large wolf eel. It is also eaten by crabs, sea otters, some birds, and people.

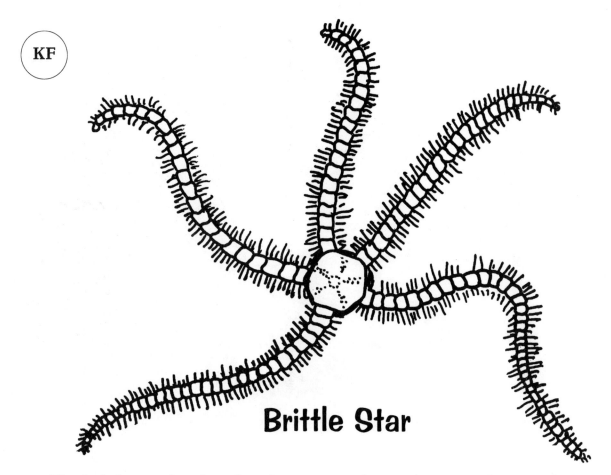

Brittle Star

The brittle star is related to the sea star. It gets its name from its fragile arms. It has five spiny, long arms, like a sea star, except that the brittle star's arms are thin and not continuous with one another like the sea star. Some brittle stars' arms are forked. Stars with these forked arms are called basket stars.

These marine invertebrates usually move very slowly, but if threatened by a predator can bend their legs and move fast. Like the sea star, if an arm is broken off, the brittle star will regenerate a new arm in its place.

Brittle stars live in shallow water, often hiding under rocks or in the mud, but they can also be found intertwined in the holdfasts of kelp. They often gather in large groups and collectively filter food from the circulating water.

Brittle stars are nocturnal, moving and feeding mostly at night. They eat decaying matter and plankton, using the many spines on their arms to filter small plankton out of the water. Some kill small animals. Like the starfish, they push their stomachs out through their mouths and digest their prey. These brittle stars are often predators or scavengers.

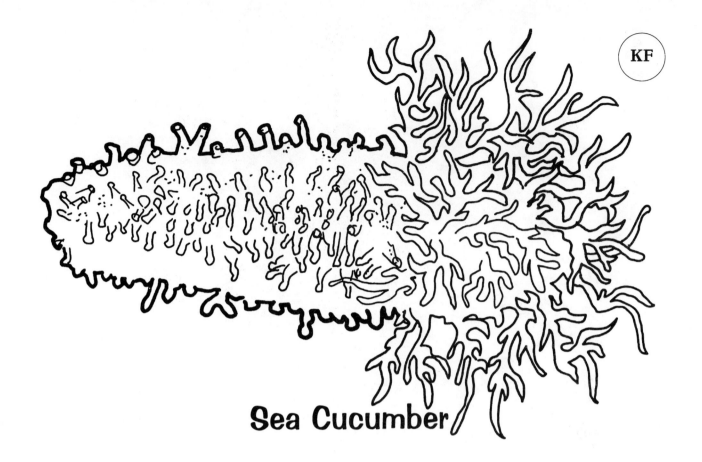

Sea Cucumber

The sea cucumber looks a lot like a sea slug, but it is related to the sea star, sea urchin and brittle star. It belongs to a class of invertebrates call echinoderms.

The sea cucumber has a long, cylindrical, cucumber-shaped body with small spines scattered along its body. On one side of its body the sea cucumber has tube feet, just like its relatives, that it uses to hang onto rocks and crawl along the mud.

The sea cucumber will often eat drifting plankton, pieces of kelp, or decaying materials that have drifted to the bottom of the sea floor. It has oral tentacles that it sticks out to capture the passing plankton.

When threatened, sea cucumbers contract their muscles and shoot out water from their body, making them shorter and harder. When scared, some can eject most of their internal organs to distract their predators. They can later regenerate a new set.

Sea cucumbers are common on the floor of the kelp forest but live in all seas and at all depths. Though most do not exceed 1 foot (30 centimeters), they can be as long as 16 inches.

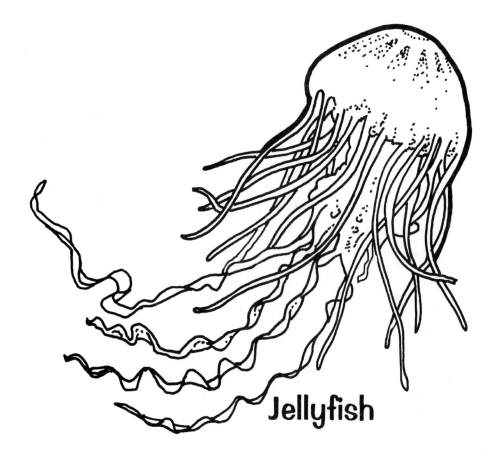

Jellyfish

Jellyfish come in all shapes and sizes; there are about 200 different varieties. These bell-shaped creatures have been around for about 600 million years. Their stinging tentacles keep many animals away from them. Jellyfish are related to sea anemones and coral, animals that also sting and have jelly-like bodies.

The body of the jellyfish is shaped like a bell or umbrella, with a filling of a jelly-like substance. The mouth is located in the center on the underside, and tentacles dangle from the edge.

The jellyfish is actually considered plankton, even though it can be very large. It is plankton because it drifts in the ocean currents. By expanding and contracting its umbrella body, it can swim up and down, but it is carried sideways in currents and waves.

Jellyfish catch their prey by using the stinging cells in their tentacles to stun or paralyze the prey. They then use the tentacles to move the food to their mouths and into their stomachs. They eat anything that comes in contact with their stinging tentacles, usually plankton, shrimp and small fish.

One of the more notorious jellyfish is the Portugese Man-of-War. It is really a colony of several individuals, each adapted to perform a different function. The tentacles of this jellyfish can be up to 60 feet (18 meters) long and can have a powerful sting that paralyzes fish and injures swimmers.

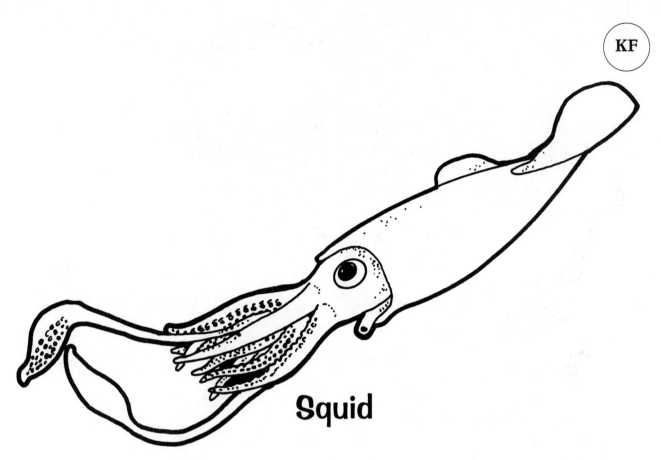

Squid

Squid are common to the kelp forest. They are members of the cephalopod class and are related to octopus and cuttlefish. All cephalopods are mollusks, invertebrates with soft bodies and a hard shell. Cephalopods are unusual, though, in that they do not have shells. The squid's shell has over time diminished to a horny plate or beak that is buried under its mantle. They range from 1 to 60 feet (.3 to 18 meters) in length.

These streamlined mollusks have a soft body and a large head (with a large brain) and can swim swiftly backwards by jet propulsion, reaching speeds of up to 20 knots (23 mph). Two fins help them stabilize their bodies while they swim. They have large eyes and ten arms (eight arms with suckers on the underside and two longer tentacles with flattened ends). The tentacles are used to seize prey.

Squid eat small fish, shrimp and plankton. They are eaten by a variety of predators, including sea otters, sea birds, large fish, sharks, humans, and sperm whales. When they are frightened, they squirt a black ink-like substance. They are also able to change color by activating special cells in their skin.

During breeding season, squid gather in huge numbers to mate and lay egg sacks in the soft muddy bottom of the kelp forest. Each female produces 10 to 50 egg strings that are attached to the ocean floor. Many females will attach their strings at the same site, making an unusual "mop" of eggs.

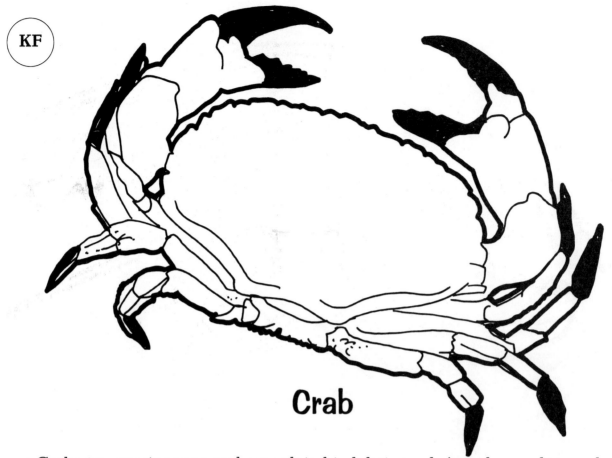

Crab

Crabs are crustaceans and are related to lobsters, shrimp, barnacles, and insects. They are covered with a hard shell called a carapace that forms from a layer of their skin. The shell protects the crab from its predators. When the crab grows too big for its shell, it wiggles out if it and a new one is made from its skin. This is called molting.

Crabs come in a variety of sizes and colors. They range in size from one centimeter to nearly two meters. Crabs have two eyes on short stalks. With their good eyesight they can see everything that is going on around them.

They have eight legs that they use for walking and two legs that are pinchers. If a crab loses a leg, it can regrow it. Crabs can run fast, usually moving sideways or backwards.

They live in many environments; mostly in sea water, but some live in fresh water and some even live on land. Different species of crabs can be found hanging on the kelp and scurrying around on the kelp forest floor. When the crab eggs are hatched, they are free-floating larva (plankton). After they grow, they settle to the ocean floor and take on the features of an adult crab.

Crabs are omnivores. Some crab are scavengers, eating dead animals and decaying material. Others eat plankton. Some young crabs eat worms, and some larger crabs eat other shellfish. Crabs are preyed upon by fish, birds, octopuses, and sea otters.

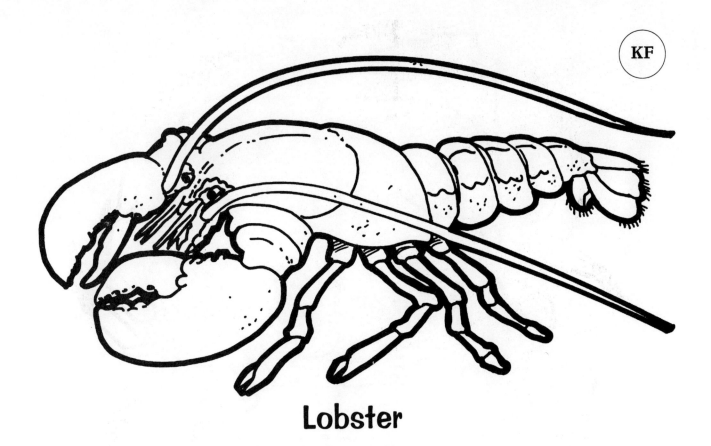

Lobster

Lobsters are marine crustaceans and are related to crabs. They have a hard exoskeleton protecting their body and five pairs of jointed legs. The first two legs are like pinchers, one larger than the other, and are used to crush the shells of their prey. A lobster's body is divided into 14 segments, and it has a movable abdomen composed of seven segments. Lobsters can be brown, blue, green or red, depending on where they live and what they eat. As the lobster grows, it sheds its exoskeleton and a new one is formed in its place.

Lobsters like to hide in the rocks at the bottom of the kelp forest. They are solitary animals, rarely gathering in groups larger than a dozen. They walk along the floor of the kelp forest and can make a quick get-away by flipping their tail under their body and shooting backwards quickly.

When the lobster's eggs hatch, they are free-swimming larva. For about a year they continue swimming, growing and molting their shells until they eventually settle to the bottom and take on the features of adult lobsters.

Lobsters are scavengers, picking up small pieces of plants and animal debris that float to the ocean floor. Occasionally a lobster will catch a passing fish in its claws, and they also prey on shellfish. Lobsters are a favorite food for seals and sea otters, as well as humans.

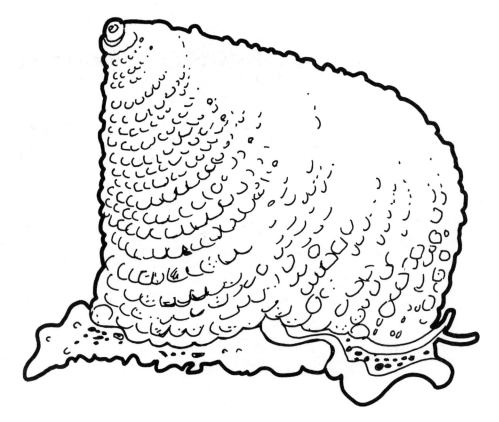

Sea Snail

The sea snail, like a garden snail, carries a large shell on its back that protects its soft body. The shell of the sea snail, however, is very thick and with a trap door called an operculum. The snail can use the operculum to close itself into its shell if it is scared or in danger.

The sea snail usually lives on hard surfaces, not on the sandy ocean bottom. It is slow-moving and uses its one strong muscular foot to keep it from getting washed off rocks by strong waves. The sea snail has a large scraping tongue called a radula. It is like a tongue with a zipper. It uses the radula to scrape algae off the rocks and to eat kelp. It has one or two pairs of tentacles that are used for sensing smells. The sea snail also has two eyes and a small brain.

While the sea snail mostly eats algae, its predators are crabs, lobsters, sea anemones, and some fish. The color of its shell depends on what it eats. As its diet changes, so does the color of its shell.

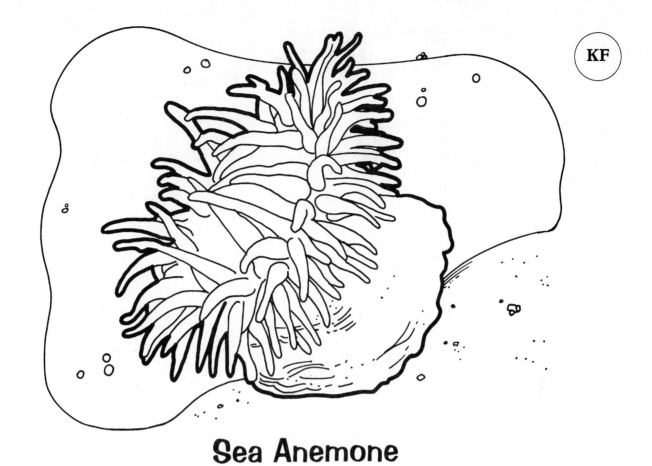

Sea Anemone

The sea anemone looks like a flower but it is a polyp and is related to coral. These organisms do not have skeletons. Sea anemones occur everywhere in the oceans. While they exist at all depths, they are abundant in coastal waters.

The sea anemone is very colorful and has several rows of tentacles surrounding its mouth. Its mouth is located on the top of its body, surrounded by its many tentacles.

Sea anemones are related to jellyfish, but they spend their lives attached to rocks and kelp. The sea anemone has stingers in its tentacles just like a jellyfish, but they are too small to hurt humans. While they spend most of their lives in one place, sea anemone's can move; but they move very, very slowly (3 to 4 inches an hour).

Sea anemones eat anything that they can catch in their stinger-filled tentacles. They often eat plankton, small crabs, small fish, and any other organisms that might fall into their reach. They often use their stinging cells (nematocysts) to immobilize their prey.

The sea anemone is a very simple animal. It does not have eyes, a brain, ears, a heart, or any complex organs. Some sea anemones can divide in half to make two new animals.

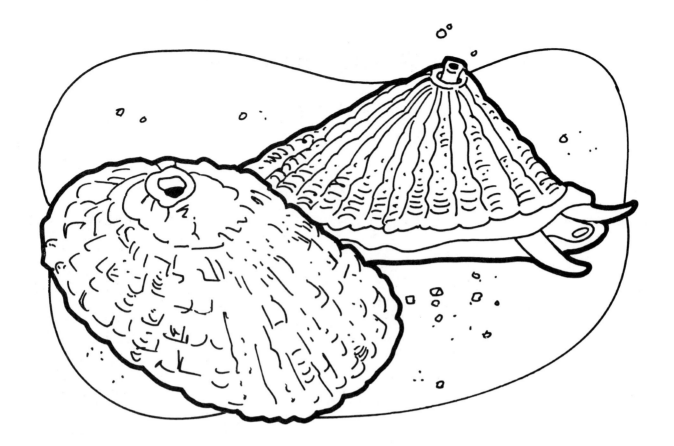

Limpet

The limpet is a relative of the snail, but has a shell shaped like a flat cone. It belongs to a group of animals called mollusks. Other animals in this group are snails, clams, mussels, oysters, octopuses, and squid.

Limpets have one big foot and a strong suction cup. Because this muscular foot is so powerful, the limpet is found in wave-swept areas where few other animals could survive. They have no eyes. They range in size from as small as a pencil eraser to as large as a dinner plate.

The limpet is found in tide pools, on the rocks, and in the kelp forests in the colder waters of the Atlantic and Pacific Oceans. The limpet eats kelp and other algae by scraping it off with its rough tongue called a radula. It eats only at night when it is safer. After it eats, it returns to the same location. Limpets will often use the same spot their entire lives.

Sea stars and birds prey on limpets. Often their shells will have bryozoans and small barnacles growing on them.

Some limpets have a hole in the top of their shell. These are called key-hole limpets.

Marine Plants and Algae

All About Algae

Background Information

Three Types of Algae

Kelp is a type of seaweed, that is, a type of algae that grows in oceans. Algae are plant-like organisms that belong to a phylum called Protista.

Algae often looks like plants, but land plants and algae are different in a few respects. Algae comes in three basic colors – red, brown and green. Kelp is a brown algae. If you visit the seashore you can often find many brown and green algae near the shore. Red algae usually grows in deeper water and is harder to find near the shore. All three types of algae contain chlorophyll and make their own food from the sun's energy through photosynthesis.

Algae is also covered with a thick protein called alginate. This sticky substance is used in many products that we find in our homes. Alginate is added to products like ice cream, cosmetics, jelly, soft cheese and toothpaste to make them thick and creamy. Kelp and other algae are harvested all over the world for these products. Kelp is also used in sushi and many other Asian foods.

Kelp Versus Other Plants

While kelp may look like a plant, there are some important differences that distinguish the two.

- Kelp has a holdfast, while a plant has roots.
- Roots are used to gather nutrients for the plant as well as to anchor it to the substrate. Kelp's holdfast does not gather any nutrients; it simply keeps the kelp anchored to the rocks.
- Plants have a system of tubes inside their stem called a vascular system. Kelp and other algae do not have a vascular system; instead kelp has a stipe.

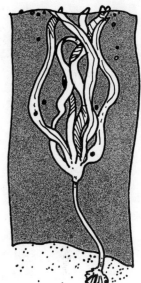

- A plant's stem is also rigid to keep it upright, where kelp's stipe is flexible.
- Kelp can absorb sunlight on both sides of its wrinkly blades and a land plant can only absorb light on one side of its smooth leaves.
- Kelp also grows very fast, up to two inches in one day.

For more information about kelp, see chapter two.

Chapter Concepts

The main focus of this chapter is learning about plants that grow in marine environments and how they are different from land plants. The concepts presented in the lessons are:

7.1 - Differences and similarities between plants and algae

7.2 - Physical analysis of algae

7.3 - Carbon dioxide/oxygen exchange

7.4 - Analysis of algae in food products

Note: *For experiments involving aquatic plants, if you use a salt water plant, be sure to use salt water in your experiment; and if you use a fresh water plant, perform the experiment with fresh water.*

Marine Plants and Algae

Activities

7.1 Algae Versus Plants

Overview

In this activity the students will compare plants and algae.

Materials

✓ "Algae Versus Plants" worksheet
✓ pencil

Procedure

1. Ask students what they know about plants that grow on land. Make a list. Introduce information about algae.

2. After you have introduced algae, give students copies of the worksheet. Have them complete it by drawing lines between the descriptions and the organisms to which they apply. Some descriptions will apply to both plants and algae.

may have formed on the sides of your aquarium is also algae. You can also find a form of algae by collecting the green scum on ponds.

2. Give students pieces of fresh algae to examine. Have them feel the texture and then look at it with a magnifying glass or microscope. If you have thin specimens and adequate magnification you can have them look for the green portions of the algae's cells. These are chloroplasts. They contain chlorophyll that enable plants to create their own food.

3. Give them a land plant and ask them to feel it, look at it, and compare it to the algae or kelp.

4. Have students complete the worksheet.

5. When the investigation of the algae is over let the students eat a piece of the algae. It will taste salty.

7.2 A Closer Look at Algae

Overview

In this activity students will observe algae using magnifying glasses or microscopes and compare it to another plant.

Materials

✓ algae
✓ land plants
✓ magnifying glasses or microscopes
✓ "Looking at Algae" worksheet

Procedure

1. Collect some algae from your local beach, buy it from a fish store, or order it through a biological supplier. The green scum that

7.3 Carbon Dioxide Cycle

Overview

This experiment introduces students to the carbon dioxide cycle that enables plants to produce oxygen that is used by fish.

Materials

✓ green fresh water plant
✓ large jar
✓ test tube
✓ funnel
✓ club soda

Procedure

1. Discuss the fact that fish need oxygen to breathe. They take in oxygen and expel carbon dioxide. Plants provide this oxygen by converting carbon dioxide.

2. Put an aquatic plant in a large jar and fill the jar with club soda that has been opened for half an hour. Invert a funnel over the jar and fill the funnel's tube with water. Fill a test tube with water and invert it over the tube of the funnel. See diagram.

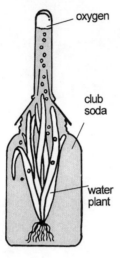

oxygen

club soda

water plant

3. Place the plant in sunlight. As the plant begins to make oxygen, the water in the test tube will be replaced with bubbles of oxygen.

7.4 Grocery Store Hunt

Overview

Students will discover what food products they use that contain algae.

Materials

✓ packaging from food, toothpaste, etc.

Procedure

1. Have students look for food with algae extracts in it. The food labels will list algae as alginate or carrageenin. They should look for it in ice cream, toothpaste, salad dressings, fruit and cereal bars, jelly, soft cheese, and cosmetics. Have students bring the containers to class.

2. Make a display with these goods and put in a place where other people in the school can view it and learn about how algae is used in food products.

If You Live by the Ocean

If you live by the ocean, schedule a trip to collect algae. In most states you do not need a permit to collect algae from the shore, but check your local regulations. Bring the algae back into the classroom for the students to investigate. If you can find an entire piece of kelp washed up on the beach with a holdfast attached, bring that back into the classroom so the students can discover what animals live inside. Make sure to return any live animals to the ocean.

Follow-up Questions/Activities

- Why is it important to have plants growing in the ocean?
- What would happen to marine animals if the marine plants died?
- What environmental threats face marine plants?
- If you live by the beach, schedule a beach clean-up day. Involve families as well as your students. This is an excellent opportunity for people to help clean the environment and for students to share what they have learned with their families.
- Buy or prepare Japanese food (like sushi) that has seaweed as one of the ingredients.
- Water plants need to be near the surface of the water where they can get ample sunlight. Design an experiment that shows that light does not pass through water as well as it does through air.
- Collect and preserve seaweed. Float the seaweed in a shallow pan. Float white paper under the seaweed. Center the seaweed on the paper and arrange the strands. Gently raise the paper out of the water and drain off the water. The gelatin in the seaweed will adhere to the paper.

Algae Versus Plants

Name _____

Draw a line from each statement to show whether it applies to algae or plants.
Some statements are true for both plants and algae.

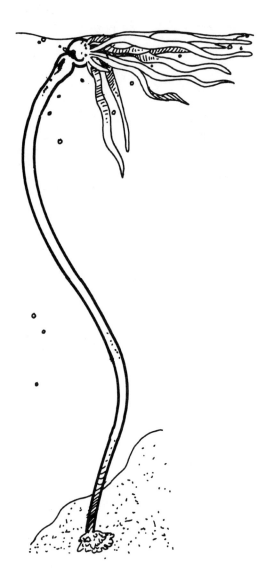

vascular system

holdfast

photosynthesis

flexible

one-sided leaves

roots

needs sunlight

chlorophyll

needs water

used in ice cream

sticky covering

lives in the air

has a stiff stem

Looking at Algae

Name _____

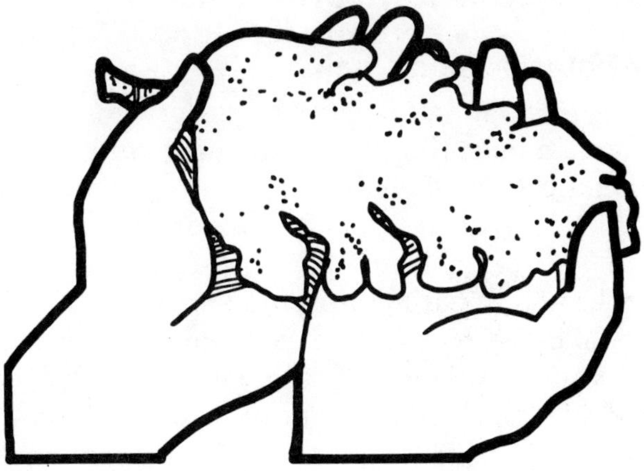

1. Describe how the algae felt.

_____
_____
_____
_____
_____

2. Draw a picture of how the algae looked.

3. How are land plants and algae different?

_____
_____
_____
_____
_____
_____

Food Chains and Webs

How Organisms Are Connected

Background Information

What is a Food Chain?

Every animal has to eat to survive, and most animals run the risk of being eaten by predators. Food chains and food webs are a tool scientists use to look at the interactions between animals and plants. A food chain looks at a linear relationship between a small set of organisms, where each animal only eats one other organism. A food web is a more complex, but realistic way of showing the relationship between many organisms that have a variety of food sources.

Producers and Consumers

A food chain always starts with the primary producer. A **primary producer** is a plant or algae that uses the sun's energy to make its own food through the process of photosynthesis. The primary producer does not have to eat anything to get energy; it makes it. An example of a primary producer is grass.

Next in the food chain is the **primary consumer.** This is the animal that eats the primary producer. Primary consumers are herbivores. An example of a primary consumer is a deer.

Next in the food chain is the **secondary** and **tertiary consumers**. The secondary consumer eats the primary consumer, and the tertiary consumer eats the secondary consumer. These animals are carnivores and omnivores. An example of a secondary consumer is a wolf.

These levels are called **trophic levels**. There may be many organisms in a food chain, each one adding to the length of the chain. Once you have constructed a food chain you can see the relationship of the organisms. Using this, you can also hypothesize what would happen to the other organisms if one were removed from the food chain. In both a food chain and a food web, arrows are drawn from an organism to another organism that eats it.

In a food web many, if not all, of the organisms in an ecosystem are represented, and the connections between prey and predator are drawn out. Since very few animals have only one source of nutrition, this is a much more realistic view of the relationships between organisms in an ecosystem. However, food webs can also get very messy with all the connections being drawn between animals, so for the purposes of this unit, we will focus on a smaller number of organisms that actually exists in an ecosystem.

Chapter Concepts

The main concept in this chapter is that organisms are interrelated. Since animals feed on smaller animals or plants, an imbalance in any level of the food chain can affect other levels. The focus of the specific lessons is:

8.1 - Introduction to food chains

8.2 - An ocean food web

8.3 - Food web simulation

8.4 - Food web simulation

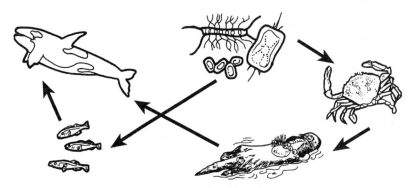

Chapter 8   # Food Chains and Webs

Activities

8.1 Food Chain

Overview

In this activity students will identify organisms by their trophic level and sequence them to create a food chain.

Materials

- ✓ "Food Chains" worksheet
- ✓ pencils

Procedure

1. Review how to use arrows to make a food chain or food web. Have students provide several examples, like the following:

    grass → rabbit → coyote

    plankton → small fish → seal

2. Give each student a copy of the worksheet. Have them write the words "producer," "primary" or "secondary" under each organism.

3. Then have them use three of the organisms to create a food chain.

8.2 Ocean Food Web

Overview

In this activity students will create a kelp forest food web and identify different organisms by their trophic level. This activity should be done after the students are familiar with the animals of the kelp forest.

Materials

- ✓ "Ocean Food Web" worksheet
- ✓ pencils

Procedure

1. Review the terms "producers," "primary consumers," "secondary consumers" and "tertiary consumers." Give examples of each one.

2. Hand out the worksheet that has kelp forest organisms arranged in a circle.

3. Have the students draw an arrow from each organism to the animal that eats it. This will be a food web.

4. After students have completed the food web, discuss which organisms are producers, primary consumers, and secondary consumers.

8.3 Food Web Simulation

Overview

In this activity students will work together to create a large ocean food web. They will also look at what happens if an animal (species) is removed from the food web.

Materials

- ✓ paper
- ✓ crayons
- ✓ string

Procedure

1. Put students into two or three groups, depending on your class size.

2. Have the students draw a picture of their favorite ocean organism. Make sure that all trophic levels are represented. You may need to assign some students to draw primary producers.

3. Have the students stand in a circle with their pictures. Connect the students with string based on what animal eats another. You have now made a food web.

4. Now take one student/organism out of the food web. What happens to the animals that ate it? What happens to the animals that it ate? See how many other organisms die out. How many become more plentiful.

8.4 Scavenging Game

Overview
This game is a simulation that depicts the change in a population of animals in terms of their camouflage characteristics.

Materials
- ✓ grassy area
- ✓ 200-400 toothpicks
- ✓ envelopes
- ✓ food coloring or tempera paint
- ✓ "Scavenger Hunt" worksheet

Procedure
1. Before you begin the game, prepare a batch of toothpicks by dyeing ¼ of them green, blue, red and yellow.

2. Take your class out onto a grassy area and explain to them that they are predatory fish trying to feed on toothpick animals that live in the kelp forest. Spread the toothpicks onto the grass and have the students stand in a line at the edge.

3. At a time signal, let the "fish" collect as much food as they can by picking up each toothpick between a thumb and forefinger and placing it in an envelope before picking up another one.

4. After 30 seconds to one minute, have the students stop hunting.

5. Count how many toothpicks of each color were picked up. Calculate how many remain and let those "reproduce" by adding

more onto the field (i.e., if 20 green remain, add 20 more green). Let the students "feed" again. You can repeat this several times.

6. Take some time before returning to the classroom to pick up as many additional toothpicks as you can find so that they will not be stepped on later. Back in the classroom, make a histogram of the results and discuss how easy or hard it was to find the different colored toothpicks. Also discuss how some animals use camouflage to hide from predators.

If You Live by the Ocean
If you live by the ocean you have the chance to observe an ocean food chain. If you take your class to the beach, have them find an animal such as a sea bird. See if they can see what the bird is eating. You can do this with as many animals as you can find. See how many different marine food chains and food webs the students can observe.

Follow-up Questions/Activities
- What happens to a food web if one animal is taken out? Are there some trophic levels that are more important than others? What would happen if all the primary producers were gone?

- Research a food web in another habitat. Focus these investigations on how all creatures in this ecosystem are connected.

- Do a small social studies unit on the Native Americans and their views on the web of life.

- Make a diagram showing a food chain that includes humans.

Food Chains

Name_____

Write the word **"producer," "primary"** or **"secondary"** under each plant or animal to tell whether each is a primary producer, primary consumer, or secondary consumer.

1. kelp

_____

2. giraffe

_____

3. bird

_____

4. tree

_____

5. cat

_____

6. sea urchin

_____

7. lion

_____

8. sea otter

_____

9. seeds or flowers

_____

10. Create a food chain. Choose three of the organisms from above and write the names in the correct order to make a food chain.

_____ ➡ _____ ➡ _____

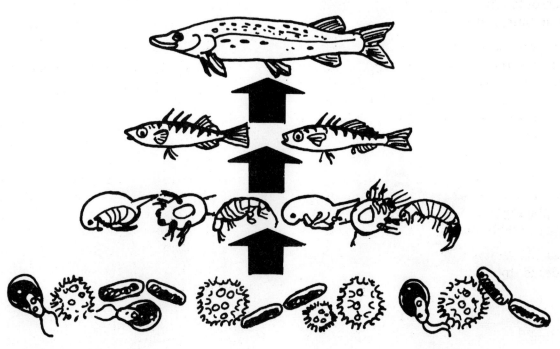

Ocean Food Web

Name _____

Connect the organisms to their predators
with arrows to create a food web.

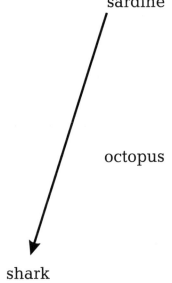

seal

kelp

sea otter

plankton

sardine

octopus

sea urchin

shark

snail

Scavenger Hunt

	orange (example)	red	blue	green	yellow
Round 1					
number at start	25				
number found	15				
left in field	10				
no. add to field	10				
Round 2					
number at start	20				
number found	6				
left in field	14				
no. add to field	14				
Round 3					
number at start	28				
number found	17				
left in field	11				
no. add to field	11				
Round 4					
number at start	22				
number found	18				
left in field	4				
no. add to field	4				
no. at end of game	8				

Glossary

Adaptation - changes in an organism in respect to its environment

Air bladder - a hollow sac filled with air; found on algae and in fish

Algae - a group of simple, plant-like organisms that use chlorophyll in photosynthesis; occurring in fresh or salt water

Antennae - movable sensory appendages occurring in pairs on the heads of some organisms

Baleen - an elastic, horny substance growing in place of teeth in the upper jaw of certain whales and forming a series of thin, parallel plates

Blade - the leaf-like structure of kelp, used to absorb light for photosynthesis

Blowhole - the opening on the top of a whale or dolphin through which it breathes

Blubber - the thick layer of fat that insulates marine mammals

Byssal threads - strong, horny threads by which the mussel attaches to the substrate

Camouflage - the act, art, or means of disguising things to deceive an enemy

Carapace - a shield covering some or all of the dorsal part of an animal

Carnivore - an animal that eats meat

Cartilage - a firm, elastic, flexible type of connective tissue

Cephalopod - the highest form of mollusks, having a head with two eyes, a beak, and tentacles, often with suckers on them

Chromatophore - a pigment cell that is capable of changing color by contracting and expanding

Crustacean - a group of animals with jointed appendages and a hard exoskeleton; includes crabs, lobster, shrimp, and barnacles

Density - the mass per unit volume of a substance

Echinoderm - a phylum of invertebrates with radial structures and hard, spiny exoskeletons; includes sea stars and sea urchins

Echolocation - the detection of an object by reflected sound; used by marine mammals

Ecology - the study of the relationships among organisms and their environment

Ecosystem - an environmental unit that consists of living and nonliving parts

Environment - the external surroundings of an organism

Estuary - marshy inlet of the ocean where it meets the end of a river

Evaporate - to change a liquid or solid into vapor; to remove the water from a substance

Exoskeleton - a hard external skeleton covering an invertebrate such as a crab

Filter feeding - a means of attaining food by filtering it out of the water using specialized appendages or organs

Flippers - the pectoral fins of marine mammals

Fluke - the caudal fin of a whale or dolphin

Fry - a young fish

Gills - organs that allows fish to extract oxygen from water

Habitat - the living place (home) of one specific organism, characterized by its physical and biological properties

Herbivore - an animal that feeds on plants

Holdfast - structure that attaches kelp to rocks; resembles a root structure

Invertebrate - an animal without a backbone

Ion - an electrically charged atom or group of atoms

Jet propulsion - the movement of a body by liquid or air being forced from it; seen in squid and lobster movement

Kelp - any large brown seaweed

Kelp forest - an aquatic environment dominated by tall kelp, a type of seaweed

Krill - a shrimp-like organism than occurs in dense swarms in polar waters; the main food of some whales

Larva - the earliest stage of development of an animal

Mammal - a large group of vertebrates in which the females have milk-secreting glands

Molecule - an element or compound consisting of one or more atoms

Mollusks - a phylum of invertebrates that typically have a soft body and a shell of one or more pieces; includes snails, octopuses, squid, bivalves, and snails

Molting - the shedding of the exoskeleton in crustaceans such as crabs

Nematocyst - an organ consisting of a small capsule containing a thread that can be ejected and cause a sting, used for protection and for catching prey

Ocean currents - the movement of large masses of water in river-like patterns in the world's oceans

Operculum - a round, hard or horny lid that closes when a snail retreats into its shell

Omnivore - an animal that eats both plants and animals

Organism - any form of plant or animal life

Phylum - the major primary subdivision of the animal kingdom (pl. - phyla)

Phytoplankton - plant plankton

Plankton - aquatic organisms that drift with water movement, usually very small

Predator - an animal that obtains energy (food) by killing and eating another organism

Primary consumer - an animal that eats plants; an herbivore

Primary producer - any plant or algae that uses the sun's energy for photosynthesis to produce its own nourishment

Radula - a rasp like organ in the mouths of mollusks used to tear up food and take it into the mouth

Salinity - a measure of the total number of dissolved solids in water

Scavenger - an animal that eats refuse and decaying matter

Schools - groups of similar animals congregating for protection, mating or feeding

Secondary consumer - an animal that eats herbivores

Species - a group of organisms that resemble each other closely and that can reproduce

Stipe - the flexible stem-like structure of kelp

Temperate - the areas between the tropics and poles with moderate water temperature and weather

Tentacles - long, slender, flexible structures used for grasping or moving

Tertiary consumer - an animal that feeds on other carnivores

Tide - the periodic rise and fall of the ocean's water due to the gravitational pull of the moon and sun

Tide pool - an area of the rocky coast where pools are formed in rock depressions during low tide

Trophic level - a step in the transfer of food or energy in a food chain or web

Tropical - a warm ocean area between the Tropic of Cancer and Tropic of Capricorn

Tube-feet - hollow tubes, many with suction-cups, used for locomotion in sea stars, sea urchins and similar animals

Vertebrate - an animal with a backbone

Zooplankton - animal plankton

Answers

From Organism to Ecosystem, pg. 15
Answers will vary.

Ecosystem Comparison, pg. 16
Answers will vary.

Water Density, pg. 22
Experiment should show that the salt water is denser than fresh water.

Floating Icebergs, pg. 23
Icebergs float because the salt falls out of the water when it freezes, leaving a fresh water iceberg. Since fresh water is less dense than salt water, the iceberg floats.

Getting to Know a Fish, pg. 31
c - protects the fish's delicate skin
d - detects odors in the water
h - a fin on the underside that helps stabilize the fish in water
a - helps fish see
g - eat and swallow water
f - another name for the tail fin
b - fin on the back of the fish
k - collects oxygen out of the water
j - this fin, along with the pelvic fin, helps stabilize the fish
i - fish use these to bite their food
e - fin near the operculum that helps fish steer when they swim

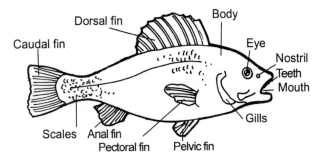

Fish Shapes, pg. 32
1. tuna
2. blue shark
3. whale shark
4. halibut
5. frog fish
6. puffer fish
1. Fast fish have streamlined, torpedo-shaped bodies that allow them to move through the water without resistence.
2. The slow fish have more rounded, less streamlined bodies.
3. ability to turn quickly, fit in tight places or eat food from cracks, poisonous, camouflage

Scales, pg. 33
2. Shark scales - like little teeth
   Bony fish - flat and rounded like a fingernail
3. Sharks feel like sandpaper in one direction and smooth in the other direction.
   Bony fish feel smooth.

Marine Mammal Traits, pg. 42
whale - a, e, i, j, k, m *   sea otter - c, f, j, k, m
seal - c, d, h, i, j, k, m   dolphin - g, i, j, k, m
walrus - d, h, i, j, k, m   manatee - b, i, k, l, m
   * g could apply for some whales

What's True . . . Mammals?, pg. 43
1. T   6. T   11. T
2. O   7. T   12. T
3. F   8. T   13. F
4. T   9. T   14. O
5. F   10. O   15. T

Algae Versus Plants, pg. 78

Algae	Plants
holdfast	vascular system
sticky coating	roots
photosynthesis	photosynthesis
flexible	flexible
one-sided leaves	lives in air
needs sunlight	needs sunlight
chlorophyll	chlorophyll
needs water	needs water
used in ice cream	stiff stem

Looking at Algae, pg. 79
Answers will vary.

Food Chains, pg. 83
1. producer
2. primary consumer
3. primary consumer
4. producer
5. secondary consumer
6. primary consumer
7. secondary consumer
8. secondary consumer
9. producer
Answers will vary.

Ocean Food Web, pg. 84

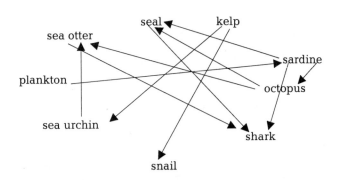